KENNETH AND VALERIE

BLOOMSBURY
GOOD READING GUIDE

TO

MURDER
CRIME FICTION
AND THRILLERS

BLOOMSBURY

First published 1990 by Bloomsbury Publishing Limited,
2 Soho Square, London W1V 5DE

Copyright © 1990 by Kenneth and Valerie McLeish

British Library Cataloguing in Publication Data

A CIP record for this book is available from the British Library

ISBN 0 7475 0732 5

10 9 8 7 6 5 4 3 2 1

Designed by Geoff Green
Typeset by Columns of Reading
Printed by Clays Ltd, St Ives plc

CONTENTS

CONTENTS

INTRODUCTION

Crime fiction was invented about 150 years ago, and almost at once took the forms it still has today. Some crime stories ('whodunnits') concentrate on detection, and show us someone puzzling out clues until the criminal (usually a murderer) is unmasked. Many of these books are romps, the author bombarding us with bizarre characters, absurd situations, ingenious murder methods and enough red herrings to sink a factory ship. Other crime stories ('whydunnits'?) focus on the criminal, and show his or her psychological state, and the circumstances which cause the crime. They tend to be far less larky than whodunnits, plunging us into the iciest, murkiest pools of the human soul.

Thrillers came later. There had been adventure stories before – such books as *Robinson Crusoe*, *The Last of the Mohicans*, *The Count of Monte Cristo* and *20,000 Leagues Under the Sea*. But true thrillers added intrigue and mystery to straightforward physical action. We never knew quite whose side everyone was on, and were as interested in the heroes' solving of that problem as in their hair's-breadth, nick-of-time escapes. The two world wars, the cold war and innumerable other twentieth-century wars gave thriller writers wonderful material. Who is 'good' and who is 'bad' in war? Where – and why – do the moral edges blur? Even as we wrote this book, the Iron Curtain collapsed all over Eastern Europe, and the politics of half our thrillers became redundant almost overnight. If the world's people are hoping to be friends, who needs spies? (No doubt thriller writers are beavering away even now, to answer this question.)

The main part of this *Guide* describes the work of 250 crime and thriller writers. We say what sort of books each writes, give some titles, and suggest follow-up reading by the same author and by others. There are also, scattered through the Guide, 'menus' of suggested reading – enjoyable books on one particular topic or another. They range from

INTRODUCTION

'Mountains' (page 113) to 'Private Eyes' (page 125), from 'Comedy thrillers' (page 29) to 'Locked-room mysteries' (page 95).

All books mentioned in the *Guide* were written in English, or are available in translation. Where a book has two titles, the UK title comes first, the US title second. We have been selective in our lists of books, preferring to give half a dozen recommendations rather than to list each author's entire output. All choices, follow-up and menu recommendations, reflect our own enthusiasms. We welcome letters, addressed to us at the publishers, with comments, suggestions and ideas, especially for 'read ons' and menus.

Although the final text is our joint responsibility, we have been assisted by many people. We should like to thank especially Pauline Fawcett, Vicki Giles, Millicent Isherwood, Andrew Langdon-Ellis, Simon McLeish, Christine McQueen, David Musson, Kate Newman, Sarah Robinson, Kathy Rooney, Stella Yates, and the tireless staff of Cambridgeshire and Lincolnshire libraries. Apart from primary sources, we found two books invaluable for dates, pseudonyms and other such information: T.J. Binyon, *Murder Will Out* and John M. Reilly (ed), *Twentieth Century Crime and Mystery Writers*. To their authors and publishers, and to everyone else who helped, much thanks.

Kenneth and Valerie McLeish
Spalding, 1990

HOW TO USE THIS BOOK

Author entries. Each author entry contains some or all of four elements:

1 a paragraph describing the author's work in general terms, sometimes by featuring a selection of books;
2 a more detailed description of one typical or outstanding book;
3 a selection of the author's other books;
4 a list of suggested 'read ons'. The 'read ons' use the symbols:

- • other book(s) by the same author
- ▶ books by other authors

Throughout the *Guide*, the symbol ▷ before a name means that that author has his or her own entry.
Authors' dates and pseudonyms. We have given these wherever possible. Some authors are reluctant to part with the information, and others were impossible to track down. Where gaps exist, we welcome assistance.
Index. The index is a useful source of follow-ups. Many of our suggestions run both ways, but the main *Guide* lists only one direction. To trace such references backwards, use the index to track down all the entries in which the book you enjoyed is mentioned. Each entry will give more follow-ups.

AIKEN, Joan • (born 1924)
English writer

Aiken, a popular children's author, also writes two kinds of adult books. First are novels of escalating psychological suspense (for example *Died on a Rainy Sunday* and *Hate Begins at Home/Dark Interval*) – they weave a terrifying atmosphere from small, unexpected shocks, with dabs of fantasy to chill the blood. Second are fast-moving, intelligent thrillers featuring women. Their heroines are alone in the world, or have had loveless, unhappy upbringings. In each novel she shows how this affects their (often bizarre) adult characters and what they do.

LAST MOVEMENT (1978)
'Mike' Meiklejohn spent the only three happy years of her childhood on the Greek island of Dendros. Now she returns to the clinic there with the mother she hardly knows, who needs psychiatric treatment. At the clinic the two women meet Lady Julia Saint, newly married after a lurid divorce – and their developing friendship is central to the book. All is not as idyllic as it seems – a sequence of gruesome murders begins. To understand what is happening, the three women must come to terms with themselves, and with their own recent and not-so-recent pasts.

Aiken's other adult books include *The Fortune Hunters*, *The Ribs of Death*, *The Embroidered Sunset* and *Trouble with Product X*.

ALLBEURY, Ted • (born 1917)
English writer

Allbeury wrote his first book when he was 54, and has

Read on

● *The Butterfly Picnic/A Cluster of Separate Sparks* (also set on Dendros, and using its mystery and beauty to similar effect).
▶ **To the novels of psychological suspense:** ▷P.M. Hubbard, *The Quiet River*; ▷Christianna Brand, *Cat and Mouse*.
▶ **To *Last Movement*:** Marion Babson, *Murder Sails at Midnight*; Rosemary Harris, *Three Candles for the Dark*.

Read on

● *A Time Without Shadows.*
▶ Duff Hart-Davis, *The*

published a dozen spy thrillers, all with cold-war settings. The action is fast and the settings are plausible (owing much to Allbeury's own career in Intelligence). Above all, the characters, on both sides, are shown as ordinary human beings, whose private lives influence their attitude to their work and to the politics which lie behind it.

Allbeury's spy stories include *A Choice of Enemies*, *Moscow Quadrille*, *The Man With the President's Mind*, *A Time Without Shadows*, *The Lantern Network*, *The Alpha List*, *The Crossing*, *Children of Tender Years* and *The Secret Whispers* (about a double agent attempting to escape from East Germany). One exception is *The Choice*, a novel about an unhappy marriage 'redeemed' by a love affair. Allbeury also uses the pseudonym 'Richard Butler' (*Where All the Girls Are Sweeter*, *Italian Assets*).

Heights of Rimring; John Lear, *Death in Leningrad*; ▷John le Carré, *The Spy Who Came in from the Cold*.

ALLINGHAM, Margery • (1905–66)
English writer

Allingham is one of the most enjoyable of all English 'golden age' writers. Her characters are wonderfully bizarre, and she has a deep love for the cobbles and back alleys of long-demolished 'village' London. Her detective, Albert Campion, conceals the obligatory razor-sharp intelligence of the detective under a vacuous, silly-ass manner, and he is at a loss neither in stories of ▷Buchanish adventure (e.g. *Sweet Danger*, *Traitor's Purse*) nor in the most uproarious of between-the-wars English farce (e.g. *The Fashion in Shrouds*; *The Beckoning Lady*).

MORE WORK FOR THE UNDERTAKER (1949)
Someone is murdering the few survivors of the eccentric Palinode family in their rabbit-warren of lodgings in Apron Street, London. What has Jas Bowels, proprietor of 'Reliable Interments', to do with it? Above all, can Mr Campion unravel the mystery in time to prevent someone else being forced to 'go up Apron Street' (whatever that sinister phrase may mean)?

Allingham's books include *Coroner's Pidgin*, *Police at the Funeral*, *Look to the Lady*, *The Tiger in the Smoke* and the short-story collections *Mr Campion and Others*, *Take Two at Bedtime* and *The Return of Mr Campion* (which also contains

 Read on

- *Flowers for the Judge* (set in a seedy 1930s London publisher's office, and involving a priceless, but unprintably pornographic manuscript); *Hide My Eyes*.
- ▷Michael Innes, *The Daffodil Affair*; ▷Edmund Crispin, *The Case of the Gilded Fly*; ▷H.R.F. Keating, *A Rush on the Ultimate*; ▷P.D. James, *A Taste for Death*.

non-Campion tales). After Allingham's death, her husband
P. Youngman Carter wrote two further Campion novels, one
of which, the thriller *Mr Campion's Farthing*, is up to his
wife's most sparkling standard.

AMBLER, Eric • (born 1909)
English writer

Ambler's novels are deadpan tales of innocent people sucked
into ever more unlikely and sinister events. His settings are
exotic (the Levant, the Far East, tropical Africa) and his plots
constantly surprising. He is a master at tightening tension
slowly but remorselessly, to release it in scenes of violence
which are short, unexpected and placed for maximum shock
effect. Films and TV pour out 'quest' thrillers by the
barrowload. But few match the pace and hypnotic urgency
which are Ambler's stock-in-trade.

THE MASK OF DIMITRIOS/COFFIN FOR DIMITRIOS
(1939)
Latimer, a writer on holiday in Smyrna, is intrigued by the
body of a criminal ('Dimitrios') in the morgue, and decides
to research the man's story. The more he investigates, and
particularly after he meets the sinister 'Mr Peters', the more
complicated and dangerous Dimitrios' story turns out to be.

Ambler's other thrillers include *Epitaph for a Spy*, *Cause for
Alarm*, *Passage of Arms*, *The Levanter*, *Doctor Frigo*, *The Schirmer
Inheritance*, *To Catch a Spy* and *Dirty Story*. Under the name
'Eliot Reed', he also wrote thrillers (e.g. *The Maras Affair*,
Charter to Danger) in collaboration with Charles Rodda.

AMES, Delano • (born 1906)
English writer

Some of Ames's books (e.g. *The Man in the Tricorn Hat*, *The
Man with Three Chins*) star Sergeant Juan Llorca of the
Spanish Guardia Civil, whose beat is a Mediterranean
fishing village. The stories are atmospheric and efficient, but
they are dwarfed by Ames's main series, a dozen comedy
thrillers starring Jane and Dagobert Brown. Dagobert is a
man of a thousand eccentric enthusiasms, whose interests
take the couple to one glamorous location after another – and

 Read on

- *The Light of Day* (about a scruffy conman forced by the Turkish police to spy on his criminal employers. Memorably filmed as *Topkapi*, starring Peter Ustinov).
- ▶ **To The Mask of Dimitrios:** Victor Canning, *The Great Affair*; ▷ Patricia Highsmith, *The Two Faces of January*; ▷ Graham Greene, *Brighton Rock*.
- ▶ **To The Light of Day:** ▷ David Dodge, *To Catch a Thief*; ▷ Lawrence Block, *Here Comes a Hero*.

 Read on

- *Murder, Maestro Please* (which takes the Browns, and the usual assortment of bizarre characters, to a Pyrenean music festival).
- ▶ ▷ Lawrence Block, *The Burglar Who Liked to Quote Kipling*; Craig

ANDERSON

always into trouble. Jane, endlessly indulgent and far more sensible, tells each story, and much of Ames's fun comes from her quizzical eye for everyone in sight, starting with her husband. Save for the Browns' Englishness, the books are exactly like 1940s American screwball comedy films, for example those starring Katharine Hepburn and Spencer Tracy.

CORPSE DIPLOMATIQUE (1950)

On the Promenade des Anglais in Nice, someone tries to shoot a Santa Rican diplomat, misses, and instead kills English expatriate Major Arkwright. The Browns, passing through on their way to Provence (where Dagobert has reasons for wanting to learn Provençal), investigate. They tangle not only with Santa Rican revolutionary politics, but also with the victims of Major Arkwright's highly successful blackmail business.

Other books in the series include *Death of a Fellow Traveller*, *The Body on Page One*, *Crime Gentlemen Please*, *Landscape With Corpse* and *Lucky Jane*.

Rice, *The Lucky Stiff*; ▷H.R.F. Keating, *The Dog It Was That Died*.

ANDERSON, J.R.L.

English writer

Anderson's main hero, Major Peter Blair, works for military intelligence in matters involving state security, and is passionate about small boats. The pace of sailing is reflected in Anderson's unhurried, unemotional style, and he supplies plentiful detail of maps, charts and timetables, leading you placidly but inexorably to the action climax of each book. The Blair books include *Death in the Thames*, *Death in the Desert*, *Death in the Caribbean*, *Death in the Greenhouse* and *Death in a High Latitude*. Anderson has also written several novels starring Chief Constable Piet Deventer. Typical is *Festival*, which begins with a pop festival, proceeds to heroin smuggling and reaches an eventful climax out at sea.

DEATH IN THE NORTH SEA (1975)

A ship's crew, investigating a body in a boat in the North Sea, is blown up by a booby-trap. Blair takes the case, uncovering a terrorist conspiracy and unwittingly instigating a kidnapping whose victim he must then rescue.

 Read on

• *Death in a High Latitude* (Blair); *A Sprig of Sea Lavender* (Deventer).
▶ ▷Andrew Garve, *The File On Lester*; ▷Geoffrey Jenkins, *Scend of the Sea*.

ANTHONY, Evelyn • (born 1928)
English writer

'Evelyn Anthony' is the pseudonym of Evelyn Ward-Thomas. She is known for historical romances (for example *Imperial Highness/Rebel Princess*; *The Heiress/The French Bride*) and for twentieth-century romantic thrillers. Her thrillers (which often involve romance between two people from different countries) include *The Tamarind Seed*, *Stranger at the Gates/The Occupying Power*, *The Persian Ransom/The Persian Prince* and *The Defector* (plus its sequel *The Avenue of the Dead*). *The Poellenberg Inheritance* (1972) is about what happens when a former Nazi general contacts his daughter to give her a priceless, looted relic – and the relic's previous owners, a wealthy and eccentric family, get to hear of it.

 Read on

- *Voices on the Wind* (about an ex-resistance worker who relives her second-world-war fight against the Nazis, her love-affairs and a betrayal).
- ▷ Mary Stewart, *Airs Above the Ground*; M.M. Kaye, *Death Walked in Cyprus*; ▷ Ted Allbeury, *The Seeds of Treason*.

THE ART OF CRIME
(painters, sculptors, forgers, murderers. . .)

Oliver Banks, *The Rembrandt Panel*
▷ Lionel Davidson, *The Chelsea Murders/Murder Games*
▷ Dick Francis, *In the Frame*
Lesley Grant-Adamson, *Guilty Knowledge*
▷ Michael Innes, *Private View/Murder is an Art*
▷ Gavin Lyall, *Venus with Pistol*
▷ Helen MacInnes, *Prelude to Terror*
▷ Charlotte MacLeod, *The Palace Guard*
▷ Minette Marin, *The Eye of the Beholder*
▷ Ngaio Marsh, *Artists in Crime*
R. Ormerod, *Still Life With Pistol*
▷ Elizabeth Peters, *Street of the Five Moons*

AVALLONE, Michael • (born 1924)
US writer

The prolific Avallone (who uses a dozen pseudonyms and has written pulp fiction of all kinds, including over 200 novels) is best known for his books about Ed Noon. Noon is a tough-talking, hard-hitting New York private eye, usually investigating messy crimes in his own backyard, but sometimes sent abroad as the president's Special Private Investigator. The style of the books is like ▷ Mickey Spillane

 Read on

▶ Robert Crais, *The Monkey's Raincoat*; ▷ Hillary Waugh, *The Glenna Powers Case*; Richard S. Prather, *Slab Happy*.

on speed, and the violence (mainly to women) is nasty and is lip-smackingly described. The best Noon books (those set in New York) include *Kill Her – You'll Like It, Lust is no Lady/The Brutal Kook, The Ultimate Client/Little Miss Murder* and *Dark on Monday* (1978), about a maniac murdering dancers in a hit Broadway musical.

B

BAGLEY, Desmond • (1923–83)
English writer

Many of Bagley's thrillers are set in Africa, and involve groups of people forced together by circumstance and battling not just outsiders and the environment but each other. In *Windfall* (1982), for example, a mysterious benefactor leaves £34 million to an obscure agricultural college in Kenya, and when Max Stafford of Stafford Security Services tries to find out why, he uncovers a writhing nest of greed, corruption and deceit. In *Juggernaut* (1985), an English adventurer leads a convoy through the war-torn state of Nyala. At the convoy's heart is a huge truck carrying the transformer for an oil-rig, and as it trundles across the countryside it becomes a mobile hospital, a battle wagon and a symbol of hope for streams of refugees, making their way to a new home somewhere beyond the war.

Bagley's other thrillers include *The Golden Keel*, *High Citadel*, *Landslide*, *The Spoilers*, *The Freedom Trap*, *Flyaway* and *Night of Error*.

Read on

- *Running Blind.*
- ▶ James Graham, *The Khufra Run*; ▷ Bob Langley, *Avenge the Belgrano*; Colin Dunne, *Black Ice*; ▷ Lionel Davidson, *The Rose of Tibet.*

BALL, John • (born 1911)
US writer

Although Ball has written thrillers (for example *The First Team* and *Mark One – The Dummy*) and 'straight' novels (for example *The Fourteenth Point*), he is best known for crime novels starring the black Californian police detective Virgil Tibbs. Tibbs uses psychological insight to solve his cases, and is particularly attuned to character-clues deduced from people's reactions to his colour. The Tibbs books begin with *In the Heat of the Night* (1965) and include *The Cool Cottontail*,

Read on

- ▶ Brian Garfield, *Relentless*; ▷ Dell Shannon, *Crime File*; K.C. Constantine, *The Rocksburg Railroad Murders.*

Five Pieces of Jade **and** *The Eyes of the Buddha*. In *Death for a Playmate/Johnny Get Your Gun* (1969) Tibbs pursues Johnny Maguire, a deprived child goaded to breaking-point by a classmate, who has shot with a real gun at the other boy's house, and then run away. The search takes Tibbs to Disneyland, to a baseball stadium where Gene Autry and his horse are appearing, and into his own understanding, based on childhood suffering at the hands of racists, of what it is to feel rejected at nine years old.

BARNARD, Robert • (born 1936)
English writer

Barnard's crime stories are as cunningly-plotted as ▷Agatha Christie's, but without a great detective: the mysteries are solved either by his likeable London policeman Perry Trethowan or by members of the local force. He is particularly good at suggesting atmosphere, whether a great house riven with family feuding, the streets of seedy Soho, or the 'typical English village' so familiar to Christie fans. His characters are sometimes stereotypes – his Cockneys tend to say 'Cor blimey' a lot – but offer a rich and lethal mixture of personalities. (He is especially good at young people.) Lastly, as in Christie, the murderer is usually the last person you suspect. Barnard's books include *Political Suicide, Posthumous Papers, Death on the High C's, A Little Local Murder* and the Trethowan novels *The Missing Brontë, Death and Princess, Sheer Torture* and *Bodies* (1986), which starts with multiple murder in the photographic studio of a body-beautiful magazine.

 Read on

- *Sheer Torture* (Trethowan); *A Corpse in a Gilded Cage* (non-Trethowan).
- Lionel Black, *A Healthy Way to Die*; D.W. Smith, *Serious Crimes*; ▷Paul Engleman, *Catch a Fallen Angel*.

BENTLEY, E(dmund) C(lerihew) • (1875–1956)
English writer

A distinguished literary critic, Bentley invented the detective Philip Trent, a languid painter-about-town with a fine line in nonsense badinage, called 'drivelling' by 1920s bright young things. Bentley's best-known book, *Trent's Last Case/The Woman in Black* (1913) is both a spoof of the great detective novel (Trent breaks every unwritten law, including falling in love with the chief suspect and getting his solution wrong), and a truly satisfying mystery, with a tortuous plot but with clues fairly placed, obvious to everyone but Trent. Bentley's other Trent books are the novel *Trent's Own Case* (in which

 Read on

- ▷Margery Allingham, *The Beckoning Lady*; ▷S.S. Van Dine, *The Scarab Murder Case*; ▷Anthony Berkeley, *Dead Mrs Stratton/Jumping Jenny*.

Trent's investigations lead him to conclude that he committed the crime himself) and the short story collection *Trent Intervenes*.

BERGMAN, Andrew
US writer

Bergman's Jack Levine books began as parodies of the private-eye novels of ▷Hammett and ▷Chandler, and are crammed with wisecracks and one-liners. But they are also suspenseful, craftily-plotted mysteries, as atmospheric as any of his models. In *The Big Kiss-off of 1944* Levine is sucked into the corrupt politics of the 1944 US presidential election and in *Hollywood and Levine* he investigates a murder in the Hollywood of Bogart, Cagney and any other tough guys and gals you care to name.

 Read on

▶ Robert Campbell, *Alice in La-la Land*; Peter Coffin, *The Search for My Great Uncle's Head*; Richard S. Prather, *Dead-Bang*; ▷Stuart M. Kaminsky, *High Midnight*.

BERKELEY, Anthony • (1893–1971)
English writer

'Anthony Berkeley' was the pseudonym of Anthony Berkeley Cox, who also wrote as ▷Francis Iles. His 18 novels simultaneously celebrate and spoof the 'fiendishly clever' detective books of the 1930s. Many of them star Roger Sheringham, an amateur, upper-class sleuth who is conceited, nosy, patronizing and highly likely to jump to completely wrong conclusions. In one book, *Dead Mrs Stratton/Jumping Jenny* (1933), we see the murder being committed, and Sheringham spends his time during the inquiry not discovering clues but planting them to confuse the police. Berkeley's witty style and his mockery of English social snobbery give his books a satirical edge as well as dazzling cleverness. He is a special taste, but a delightful one.

Berkeley's Sheringham novels include *The Poisoned Chocolates Case, Top Storey Murder, Murder in the Basement* and *Panic Party/Mr Pidgeon's Island*. His other crime novels include *The Piccadilly Murder, Not to be Taken/A Puzzle in Poison* and *Death in the House*.

 Read on

● *Trial and Error.*
▶ ▷Francis Iles, *Malice Aforethought*; ▷E.C. Bentley, *Trent's Last Case/The Woman in Black*; Kingsley Amis, *The Riverside Villas Murder*; ▷S.S. Van Dine, *The Bishop Murder Case*; ▷Patrick Quentin, *The Wife of Ronald Sheldon/My Son the Murderer*.

BIG MONEY

▷Bob Cook, *Disorderly Elements*
▷David Dodge, *Shear the Black Sheep*
▷M.G. Eberhart, *Danger Money*
▷Stanley Ellin, *Very Old Money*
▷Paul Erdman, *The Silver Bears*
▷Joseph Hansen, *Death Claims*
▷Emma Lathen, *Double, Double, Oil and Trouble*
  Lawrence Sanders, *The Timothy Files*
  M.M. Thomas, *Ropespinner Conspiracy*
▷John Trenhaile, *The Mahjong Spies*
▷Donald E. Westlake, *Bank Shot*

BLAISDELL, Anne
see LININGTON, Elizabeth

BLAKE, Nicholas • (1904–72)
Irish writer

'Nicholas Blake' was the pseudonym of C. Day Lewis. He wrote 20 detective novels, many of them starring the amiable amateur sleuth Nigel Strangeways. The books are in true British 'golden age' crime style. Wherever Strangeways goes – on a Greek cruise, to a London publishing house, to the Ministry of Information at the end of the second world war – gruesome murder is committed, and Strangeways solves it by patiently getting acquainted with a large group of eccentric and extraordinary people. The books are leisurely, full of 'good literary talk' and inconsequential banter: like many English upper-class detectives, Strangeways loves concealing his education – or showing it off – by talking frivolous nonsense. Blake's books, underrated nowadays, are worth discovering.

The Strangeways books (which should be read in chronological order, as they follow his life from university to middle age) include *A Question of Proof, Thou Shell of Death, The Beast Must Die, The Smiler With the Knife, Malice in Wonderland/The Summer Camp Mystery/Malice With Murder, End of Chapter* and *The Worm of Death*. Blake's non-Strangeways thrillers include *A Tangled Web/Death and Daisy Bland, A Penknife in my Hand* and *The Deadly Joker*.

 Read on

▶ ▷Edmund Crispin, *Holy Disorders*; ▷Ngaio Marsh, *Final Curtain*; ▷Margery Allingham, *Flowers for the Judge*.

BLAKE, Patrick
see EGLETON, Clive

BLEECK, Oliver
see THOMAS, Ross

BLOCH, Robert • (born 1917)
US writer

Bloch began his career at 17, writing horror short stories for the magazine *Weird Tales*. In the 1940s he began to publish psychological suspense novels: chillers about psychopaths, religious fanatics, child-molestors and arsonists. His best known book, thanks to Hitchcock's film, is *Psycho* (1959), but his other novels are equally sure to freeze the blood. Particularly recommended are *The Scarf, Firebug, Nightworld* and *Terror*.

 Read on

▶ ▷ John Katzenbach, *The Traveller*; ▷ Ira Levin, *A Kiss Before Dying*; ▷ Pierre Boileau and Thomas Narcejac, *Choice Cuts*.

BLOCK, Lawrence • (born 1938)
US writer

Block's best known books are two series of comedy thrillers. The Evan Tanner books (for example *The Cancelled Czech, Here Comes a Hero, Me Tanner, You Jane*) are among the most relaxed and best of James Bond spoofs. The Bernie Rhodenbarr books (for example *Burglars Can't Be Choosers, The Burglar Who Liked to Quote Kipling, The Burglar Who Studied Spinoza*) are crime capers about a New York bookshop owner who is a burglar in his spare time. *Deadly Honeymoon* and *The Specialists* are non-series caper novels. Under the pseudonym 'Chip Harrison' (republished under his own name) Block has written splendid ▷ Rex Stout spoofs, including the magnificently-named *The Topless Tulip Caper*.

 Read on

● *The Thief Who Couldn't Sleep.*
▶ ▷ Donald E. Westlake, *Help! I Am Being Held Prisoner*; ▷ John Godey, *The Reluctant Assassin/A Thrill A Minute with Jack Albany*; ▷ Delano Ames, *Corpse Diplomatique*; ▷ Pamela Branch, *Murder's Little Sister*.

BOATS, SHIPS AND SUBMARINES

▷ J.R.L. Anderson, *Death in the Thames*
  Marian Babson, *Murder Sails at Midnight*
▷ John Dickson Carr, *The Blind Barber*
▷ Freeman Wills Crofts, *The Loss of the Jane Vosper*

BOILEAU

Paul Gallico, *The Poseidon Adventure*
▷Andrew Garve, *Came the Dawn*
▷Geoffrey Jenkins, *Scend of the Sea*
▷Alistair MacLean, *HMS Ulysses*
▷Philip McCutchan, *Cameron's Chase*
Melville Ross, *Trigger*
▷Wilbur Smith, *Hungry is the Sea*
E.E. Vielle, *The Shadow of Kuril*

BOILEAU, Pierre and NARCEJAC, Thomas
French writers

In the 1950s and 1960s Boileau and Narcejac had international success with a series of macabre thrillers, suspense-webs spun from madness, remorseless evil and the supernatural. Their novels include *The Woman Who Was*, *The Living and the Dead*, *Heart to Heart*, *Spells of Evil* and *Choice Cuts* (1965), a terrifying black comedy in which the body of an executed criminal is cut up and grafted (in parts) on to seven people maimed in car crashes – and then decides that it wants to be reunited with itself again.

BOUCHER, Anthony • (1911–68)
US writer

'Anthony Boucher' was the pseudonym of the critic, editor and reviewer W.A.P. White. He specialized in tongue-in-cheek stories of 'impossible' crimes, with delightfully elaborate settings. *The Case of the Baker Street Irregulars/Blood on Baker Street* (1940) and *The Case of the Solid Key* (1941) are set in Hollywood. In the first, Boucher's detectives, O'Breen and Jackson, investigate a murder during the making of a Sherlock Holmes film, and in the second they have to solve a locked-room mystery with a cast of easily-recognizable film stars as suspects. In two other novels, *Nine Times Nine* (1940) and *Rocket to the Morgue* (1941), the crimes are locked-room mysteries and the detective is Sister Ursula, a Roman Catholic nun.

Boucher's other O'Breen and Jackson novels are *The Case of the Crumpled Knave* and *The Case of the Seven Sneezes*.

 Read on

• *The Prisoner* (about an escaped prisoner of war in occupied France who is not all he claims to be – and who finds that his wife, too, is playing a macabre game).
▶ John Blackburn, *A Ring of Roses*; H.G. Wells, *The Island of Doctor Moreau*; ▷Helen McCloy, *The Slayer and the Slain*.

Read on

▶ To the Hollywood novels: ▷John Dickson Carr, *The Three Coffins* (locked-room); Cameron McCabe, *The Face on the Cutting Room Floor* (film business); ▷Andrew Bergman, *Hollywood and Levine* (Hollywood).

BOULLE, Pierre • (born 1912)
French writer

Boulle wrote two dozen novels, many about colonists, planters and revolutionaries in the Far East during the earlier years of this century. He is best known for two 1960s books which were made into blockbuster films: *Bridge on the River Kwai* (a psychological suspense story set in a second-world-war Burmese prison camp) and *Planet of the Apes* (a science fiction adventure set on a planet inhabited by intelligent monkeys). His other books include *The Executioner/The Chinese Executioner*, *The Other Side of the Coin* and *Ears of the Jungle*. *Time Out of Mind* is a collection of short stories.

 Read on

- *The Virtues of Hell* (about a drug-addicted war-veteran, branded a coward, whose quest for a way to refine pure heroin eventually takes him back to the jungle to face, and defeat, his fear).
- ▷C.S. Forester, *The African Queen*; Joseph Conrad, *Typhoon*; Paul Theroux, *The Mosquito Coast*.

BOX, Edgar
see VIDAL, Gore

BRAHMS, Caryl and SIMON, S.J.
English writers

'Caryl Brahms' was the pseudonym of Doris Caroline Abrahams (1901–82). With S.J. Simon (1903–47), who preferred not to reveal his first names, she wrote a dozen crazily funny novels, including *No Bed For Bacon* (spoofing Shakespeare) and *Don't, Mr Disraeli* (spoofing Victorian England). They also wrote three books entangling mild-mannered, terminally nice Inspector Adam Quill with the Russian ballet company run by Vladimir Stroganoff. The novels are *A Bullet in the Ballet*, *Casino for Sale/Murder à la Stroganoff* and *Six Curtains for Stroganova/Six Curtains for Natasha*. They are wild farces, similar in style to 1930s American screwball comedy films, and have ridiculous characters, lunatic situations and preposterous, pun-filled dialogue. Who killed Petrushka? Who cares? Enjoy the show!

Brahms and Simon wrote one other Quill book, *Envoy on Excursion*, a spy-quest spoof set in the second world war. Their other comedies include *No Nightingales* and *Titania Had a Mother*.

 Read on

- ▷Pamela Branch, *Murder Every Monday*; ▷Charlotte MacLeod, *Vane Pursuit*; Craig Rice, *The Big Midget Murders*.

BRAMAH, Ernest • (1868–1942)
English writer

Detective short stories are rare, and Bramah's Max Carrados

 Read on

- ▷G.K. Chesterton, *The Innocence of Father*

stories are among the best. Carrados is a blind, rich amateur who works out mysteries in his study, while his partner, the inquiry agent Louis Carlyle, does the leg work – a similar situation to that of ▷Rex Stout's Wolfe and Goodwin. Bramah is worth mentioning in the same breath as Stout both for the ingenuity of his mysteries and the elegance and wit of the telling.

Bramah's Carrados stories are collected in *Max Carrados, The Eyes of Max Carrados* and *The Specimen Case. The Bravo of London* is a full-length Carrados novel. Bramah is also known for eight books of gentle, mock-Chinese tales told as if by a village story-teller, Kai Lung.

Brown; ▷Rex Stout, *Justice Ends at Home;* ▷Margery Allingham, *Mr Campion and Others.*

BRANCH, Pamela
English writer

Branch's larky comedy-thrillers, popular in the 1950s, are now unjustly neglected. They are brisk, black farces, brilliantly described by one reviewer as 'ghoulish soufflés'. In *Murder Every Monday* (1954), a gang of 'resting' assassins runs a residential course in murder, with deadly results. In *Murder's Little Sister* (1958), the universally-loathed agony aunt of a women's magazine is almost murdered, and responds by causing so much havoc that the question becomes not 'Whodunnit?' but 'Who will do it – please, and soon?'.

 Read on

● *Lion in the Cellar; The Wooden Overcoat.*
▶ ▷H.R.F. Keating, *Zen There Was Murder;* Peter Anthony, *The Woman in the Wardrobe;* ▷Donald E. Westlake, *Two Much!*

BRAND, Christianna ● (1909–88)
English writer

Brand is best known for her novels starring the country policeman Inspector Cockrill. Presented with a tangle of suspects and motives, he unravels it with a mixture of dogged investigation and psychological acuteness which make Poirot look dim. Brand also wrote several fine non-Cockrill novels, including the gothic thriller *Cat and Mouse* (1950), which begins as a magazine agony aunt travels to rural Wales to visit one of her most persistent and anguished correspondents – only to find that the woman does not exist.

Brand's Cockrill novels include *Heads You Lose, Green For Danger, London Particular/Fog of Doubt* and *The Three-*

 Read on

▶ **To the Cockrill books:**
▷W. J. Burley, *To Kill a Cat.*
▶ **To *Cat and Mouse*:**
▷P.M. Hubbard, *A Thirsty Evil;* ▷Helen McCloy, *The Impostor;* ▷Julian Symons, *The Thirty-First of February.*

Cornered Halo. Her non-Cockrill thrillers include *Death in High Heels, Court of Foxes* and *A Ring of Roses* (originally published under the pseudonym 'Mary Ann Ashe'). *What Dread Hand?* and *Brand X* are collections of sprightly short stories.

BRETT, Simon • (born 1945)
English writer

Brett's Charles Paris comedy mysteries are set in the worlds of theatre, television, film and radio. Paris is a (deservedly) unsuccessful actor, one of that large pool of 'pros' who keep up appearances while hoping for small parts to turn up. From time to time they do – as do the murders Paris investigates. Brett has a different 'backstage' setting for each book: the Edinburgh Festival (*So Much Blood*), the BBC (*Dead Side of the Mike*), the musical stage (*Star Trap*). He is wickedly funny about human and institutional foibles, and his accounts of the reaction of the secure middle class to the vagabond freelance life – a feature of the Paris stories – are even tarter in books featuring Mrs Pargeter (for example *A Nice Class of Corpse, Mrs Presumed Dead*). She is the mystery-solving rich widow of a man whose profession is never mentioned but who had a large circle of useful, if shady, acquaintances.

WHAT BLOODY MAN IS THAT? (1987)
Writing about an under-rehearsed production of *Macbeth*, Brett enjoys being sharp about subsidized theatre, stage-struck beginners, the slackness of old hands, the weakness of directors and the effects of sit-com on acting techniques. The murder is casually, almost reluctantly introduced, and Paris is the prime suspect until he solves the case.

Brett's Paris books include *Cast, In Order of Disappearance, A Comedian Dies, Situation Tragedy* and *Murder Unprompted.*

BUCHAN, John • (1875–1940)
English writer

Buchan wrote more than 100 books, of which two dozen thrillers are nowadays the best known. There are three series, starring respectively: gentleman-of-action Richard Hannay; Glasgow shopkeeper Dickson McCunn; and lawyer

 Read on

● *Dead Side of the Mike.*
▶ Jane Dentinger, *Murder on Cue*; ▷H.R.F. Keating, *Death of a Fat God*; Tim Heald, *Let Sleeping Dogs Lie* ('backstage' among dog-breeders).

 Read on

● *Greenmantle.*
▶ Erskine Childers, *The Riddle of the Sands*; ▷Geoffrey Household, *Rogue Male*; W. Somerset Maugham, *Ashenden.*

Sir Edward Leithen (the Leithen books are the most serious and psychologically 'deep'). The basic formula is always the same. The hero is told about, or stumbles upon, a Conspiracy to 'End Civilisation as We Know It', and sets out single-handed, or with the help of a few trusted friends, to frustrate it. He is chased (often by the police as well as by the criminals), and wins through by a combination of physical courage and absolute moral certainty. The pleasure of Buchan's novels is enhanced by the magnificently described wild countryside he sets them in (usually the Scottish highlands or the plains of southern Africa), and by their splendid minor characters – the shopkeepers, tramps, local policemen and landladies who help his heroes, often at enormous personal risk.

THE THIRTY NINE STEPS (1915)

Hannay, returning from South Africa, is told by a chance American acquaintance of a plot to invade England. Soon afterwards the American is killed and Hannay is framed for his murder. To escape two manhunts, one by the conspirators and the other by the police, he takes to the hills, and only after 300 pages of breathtaking peril does he succeed in saving his country and clearing his name.

Buchan's other Hannay thrillers are *Greenmantle, Mr Standfast, The Three Hostages, The Courts of the Morning* and *The Island of Sheep*. His McCunn books are *Huntingtower, Castle Gay* and *House of the Four Winds*. His Leithen novels are *The Power House, John MacNab, The Dancing Floor, Gap in the Curtain, The Runagates Club* and *Sick Heart River/Mountain Meadow*. Other novels include *Prester John, Witchwood* and *The Blanket of the Dark*.

BURLEY, W(illiam) J(ohn) • (born 1914)

English writer

Burley's Superintendent Wycliffe is a ruminative, pipe-smoking detective – an English Maigret, except that instead of working in a city he solves cases in the towns and placid countryside of Cornwall. He likes to soak himself in the atmosphere of a place, watching and waiting as each case evolves – and this is satisfyingly balanced, again as with Maigret, by the tension and hysteria (often involving sex) which underlie the crimes. The Wycliffe books include *To Kill a Cat, Guilt Edged, Death in Stanley Street, Wycliffe and the*

 Read on

- *Wycliffe and the Scapegoat.*
- ► George Bellairs, *Littlejohn on Leave;* Anthea Fraser, *Pretty Maids All in a Row;* ▷Roy Lewis, *Error of Judgement;* Gil North, *Sergeant Cluff Stands Firm.*

Schoolgirls and *Wycliffe in Paul's Court*. Burley has also written books starring the zoologist and amateur sleuth Henry Pym (*A Taste of Power*, *Death in Willow Pattern*), and several non-series psychological novels (mystery rather than crime) including *The Sixth Day*, *Charles and Elizabeth* and the brooding *The Schoolmaster*, about a teacher who falls in love with a sexually precocious pupil who subsequently dies.

BURNETT, W(illiam) R(iley) • (1899–1982)

US writer

Burnett wrote films during Hollywood's 1930s-40s 'golden age', and published over 50 books, chiefly westerns and crime thrillers. He wrote two of the best known crime novels of the century. *Little Caesar* (1929), later magnificently filmed with Edward G. Robinson, is the story of Rico, a small-time Chicago gangster who bullies, betrays and kills his way to the top during Prohibition, only to fall. *The Asphalt Jungle* (1949) is one of the first, and best, 'caper' novels, following in detail the progress of a spectacular crime.

 Read on

- *High Sierra* (about an escaped murderer); *The Widow Barony* (a larky story about a beautiful widow causing emotional and political havoc in a banana republic Caribbean dictatorship).
- ▶ To *Little Caesar*: Mario Puzo, *The Godfather*; ▷Donald E. Westlake, *The Mercenaries/The Smashers*.
- ▶ To *The Asphalt Jungle*: Lionel White, *The Big Caper*.
- ▶ To Burnett's work in general: ▷James M. Cain, *The Postman Always Rings Twice*; Ernest Hemingway, *To Have and Have Not*.

BUTLER, Gwendoline • (born 1927)

English writer

Under her own name, Butler has written a series of novels about Inspector Coffin of the CID – plainly-told but meaty stories in which investigating the murder usually leads Coffin to unravel some far more tangled mystery. Save that her hero is a policeman and her milieu is contemporary London, Butler's books are close in structure and ideas to ▷Ross Macdonald's Lew Archer novels. All the Coffin books have the word 'Coffin' in the title. (*A Coffin for Pandora/Olivia* is the exception – a non-Coffin novel, a superb police procedural set in 1880s Oxford.) Under the pseudo-

 Read on

- ▶ ▷Reginald Hill, *An Advancement of Learning*; ▷Roy Lewis, *A Question of Degree*; ▷Colin Dexter, *Last Seen Wearing*.

nym 'Jennie Melville', Butler has written a second series of police procedurals, starring policewoman Charmian Daniels, and a number of romantic crime thrillers including the atmospheric *Nun's Castle*, *Raven's Forge* and *Axwater/Tarot's Tower*.

Butler's Coffin books include *Coffin in Oxford*, *Coffin in Malta*, *A Coffin from the Past* and *A Coffin for the Canary*. Melville's Daniels books include *Come Home and Be Killed*, *Murderers' Houses* and *There Lies Your Love*.

BUTLER, Richard
see ALLBEURY, Ted

CAIN, James M(allahan) • (1892–1977)
US writer

Cain's *The Postman Always Rings Twice* (1934) is a bitter story about two no-hopers in Depression Hollywood who become entangled in escalating, violent crime. The book is exactly in the style of those black-and-white, rain-soaked crime melo-dramas Hollywood was turning out in the 1930s, and has itself been filmed several times. It overshadows the rest of Cain's output, which is equally bleak, equally matter-of-fact about sex and violence, and equally exciting. His best books are *Serenade, The Butterfly, Jealous Woman, The Magician's Wife* and *Three of a Kind* (a collection of three short novels, one of which, 'Double Indemnity', is his masterpiece, as good as any of ▷Simenon's psychological thrillers).

 Read on

▶ Horace McCoy, *No Pockets in a Shroud*; Cornell Woolrich, *The Bride Wore Black/Beware the Lady*; ▷Georges Simenon, *The Man Who Watched the Trains Go By*; ▷Richard Stark, *Point Blank/The Hunter*.

CANDY, Edward • (born 1925)
English writer

'Edward Candy' is the pseudonym of Alison Neville, who has written eight non-crime novels, and three detective stories. In these, amateurs, notably the large, jolly paedia-trician Fabian Honeychurch, help temperamental Inspector Burnivel solve the crimes. One of the books' main pleasures is the delight Candy takes in describing the atmosphere and location of each investigation: a children's hospital in *Which Doctor*, the Royal College of Paediatricians in *Bones of Contention* and crime fiction evening classes in *Words for Murder, Perhaps*. In these books, as in all Candy's writing, the prose is richly-textured, the characters are drawn in great psychological depth, and the mixture of hilarity and the macabre is superb.

 Read on

▶ ▷Amanda Cross, *In the Last Analysis*; ▷P.D. James, *Shroud for a Nightingale*; ▷Peter Dickinson, *Perfect Gallows*.

CAPERS

▷Eric Ambler, *The Light of Day*
  Richard Barth, *A Ragged Plot*
▷Lawrence Block, *Deadly Honeymoon*
▷W.R. Burnett, *The Asphalt Jungle*
▷Jon Cleary, *Peter's Pence*
▷Richard Condon, *Arigato*
▷James Follett, *Swift*
  Allan Prior, *The Operators*
▷Lawrence Sanders, *Caper*
▷Donald E. Westlake and ▷Brian Garfield, *Gangway!*

CARR, John Dickson • (1906–77)
US writer

Carr also wrote novels under the pseudonym ▷'Carter Dickson' – ideal follow-ups to his books under his own name. These include two dozen starring Doctor Gideon Fell, an eccentric scholar with the brains of a Mycroft Holmes and a Falstaffian gusto for food, beer and pipe-tobacco. Fell's hobby is solving such 'impossible' crimes as locked-room mysteries. The stories are tightly plotted, the mysteries ingenious, and Fell's character, if a bit old bufferish for late-twentieth-century tastes, is fascinating. Carr also wrote historical detective novels, set in eighteenth- or nineteenth-century England.

HAG'S NOOK (1933)
Hag's Nook is the tower of an eighteenth-century prison, not far from Dr Fell's cottage in the English countryside. Every male heir in the original governor's family must spend one hour in Hag's Nook just before midnight on his 25th birthday – and risk being found next morning with a broken neck. When the latest heir is found dead it is for Dr Fell to find out whether a ghost or a common-or-garden murderer haunts the tower, and why.

Carr's Doctor Fell books include *The Blind Barber*, *The Case of the Constant Suicides*, *Till Death Us Do Part* and *The House at Satan's Elbow*. His historical novels include *The Bride of Newgate*, *The Devil in Velvet*, *The Witch of the Lowtide*, *Fire Burn!* and *Scandal at High Chimneys* (in which the detective is

 Read on

● *The Seat of the Scornful* (did Judge Ireton, found sitting by the body with a smoking gun in his hand, really murder his daughter's unsuitable fiancé?).
▶ **To *Hag's Nook*:** ▷Margery Allingham, *Look To the Lady*; ▷Michael Innes, *Lament for a Maker*.
▶ **To Carr's Dr Fell books in general:** ▷Rex Stout, *Where There's a Will*; Craig Rice, *Trial by Fury*.
▶ **To Carr's historical stories:** ▷Wilkie Collins, *The Woman in White*; Jeffery Farnol, *The High Adventure*; Jeremy Sturrock, *The Wilful Lady*.

no less a personage than ▷Wilkie Collins). He also wrote several books starring the French detective Bencolin: they include *It Walks by Night* and *The Waxworks Murder/The Corpse in the Waxworks*. His collections of short stories include *The Men Who Explained Miracles* and *The Exploits of Sherlock Holmes*.

CARTER, P. Youngman

see ALLINGHAM, Margery

CASPARY, Vera • (born 1904)
US writer

Read on

- *The Husband.*
- ▷Winston Graham, *Marnie*; Mary Carter Roberts, *Little Brother Fate*; ▷Ruth Rendell, *A Demon in My View*.

Caspary's psychological mysteries grip by the second paragraph and never let go. She buttonholes us emotionally, writing swift clipped prose with particularly punchy dialogue (a legacy from years of film work). Her chief skill is letting us inside the minds of her characters, particularly daydreamers and those whose personality is dominated by a single feeling (love, fear, jealousy) to an all but pathological extent.

THE MAN WHO LOVED HIS WIFE (1966)
Fletcher J. Strode, an ebullient, vital man, is devoted to his wife Elaine. When his larynx is removed because of cancer he is unable to cope. Feelings of inadequacy are compounded by paranoid jealousy of every man to whom his wife speaks. His diary tells how he first plans suicide, then begins to fantasize, first that Elaine wants him to kill himself, then that she intends to kill him herself. When he dies, the diary remains as evidence. Superb character-drawing, not only of Strode himself, but of such minor characters as an ambitious, vain policeman, Strode's daughter and her weak-willed husband.

Caspary's books include *Laura, Stranger Than Truth, Thelma, Bedelia, A Chosen Sparrow, Final Portrait* and *Ruth*.

CHANDLER, Raymond • (1888–1959)
US writer

Read on

- *The Big Sleep; The Lady in the Lake.*
- ▷Dashiell Hammett, *The Maltese Falcon*; ▷Ross MacDonald, *The Drowning Pool*; ▷Robert

Chandler said that his ambition was to replace the kind of detective stories fashionable in the 1930s (tales of bizarre crimes solved by wildly eccentric detectives, distantly modelled on Sherlock Holmes) with books about realistic crimes, investigated in a believable way by a detective who would be ordinary, with recognizable human hopes, fears and failings. Philip Marlowe (Chandler's private eye) is an honest, conscientious man who sweats, cowers and lusts just like anyone else. He narrates the stories himself, in a deadpan style – 'The next morning was bright, clear and sunny. I woke up with a motorman's glove in my mouth, drank two cups of coffee and went through the morning papers' – which is brilliantly caught in the performances of two actors who have played Marlowe most successfully on film, Humphrey Bogart and Dick Powell. Few writers have ever matched Chandler's sense of atmosphere and of the moral corruption which lies just under the skin of life. This feeling of teetering on the edge of one new chasm of human awfulness after another has been imitated by virtually every private-eye writer since Chandler's time, and it is one of the main pleasures of his work.

FAREWELL, MY LOVELY (1940)

Marlowe is drifting with nothing particular to do when he is picked up (literally, by the scruff of the neck) by a musclebound ex-convict called Moose Malloy. From this simple event, as ripples spread on a pond, the story grows to take in a priceless necklace, kidnapping, blackmail and murder. At its heart, like a man in the still centre of a whirlwind, Marlowe slouches from clue to clue, pushing open every door and investigating each alleyway even though he knows, from long experience, that he's likely to find painful or nasty surprises at every turn.

Chandler's novels are *The Big Sleep*, *Farewell My Lovely*, *The High Window*, *The Lady in the Lake*, *The Little Sister*, *The Long Goodbye* and Playback. His unfinished Marlowe novel, *Poodle Springs*, was completed by ▷Robert B. Parker in 1989. *Killer in the Rain* is a collection of short stories.

CHARTERIS, Leslie • (born 1907)

US writer

Charteris' character Simon Templar, 'The Saint', is a twentieth-century Robin Hood, an adventurer who rights wrongs, puts down the pompous, exposes frauds, rescues damsels in distress – and relieves crooks of their ill-gotten, excess cash. Charteris' 1930s books, set in England, show the Saint in criminal circles, constantly one step ahead of

B. Parker, *Playmates*;
▷John Milne, *Shadow Play*.

 Read on

▶ **To Charteris' 1930s books:** E.W. Hornung, *The Amateur Cracksman/Raffles*, the Amateur Cracksman (and more Raffles stories by Barry Perowne, for example

plodding Inspector Teal of Scotland Yard. In later books, the Saint is based in the USA, and is an international trouble-shooter, a kind of unlicensed, freelance James Bond.

Charteris' 1930s Saint books include *The Last Hero*/*The Saint Closes the Case*, *The Saint in New York* and *The Saint Goes West*. His later books include *Send for the Saint* and *The Saint and the Templar Treasure*. There are two dozen books of short stories, all with the word 'Saint' in the title, and many omnibuses.

Raffles After Dark/*The Return of Raffles*); ▷John Creasey, *Introducing the Toff*.
▶ **To his later books:** Louis J. Vance, *Red Masquerade*.

CHASE, James Hadley • (born 1906)
English writer

 Read on

▶ ▷James M. Cain, *The Postman Always Rings Twice*; ▷Michael Avallone, *Kill Her – You'll Like It*; Norman Mailer, *Tough Guys Don't Dance*.

'James Hadley Chase' is one of the pseudonyms of René Brabazon Raymond. He is the author of 100 gangster thrillers, most of them set in the USA – violent, hard-talking equivalents of the Hollywood gangster films of the 1940s. His best known book is *No Orchids for Miss Blandish*/*The Villain and the Virgin* (1939), about the search for a kidnapped heiress. Under a second pseudonym, 'Raymond Marshall', Raymond wrote thrillers starring the private eye Brick-Top Corrigan, as tough as flint, and the millionaire adventurer Don Micklem.

CHESTERTON, G(ilbert) K(eith) • (1874–1936)
English writer

 Read on

▶ **Crime short stories:** ▷Arthur Conan Doyle, *The Adventures of Sherlock Holmes*; R. Austin Freeman, *The Singing Bone*.
▶ **Novels where a detective uses the thought-patterns of his religion to solve crimes:** ▷Harry Kemelman, *Friday the Rabbi Slept Late* (Talmud); ▷James Melville, *The Wages of Zen* (Zen Buddhism).

Chesterton published over 200 books – essays, poetry, criticism, biographies, works on Christianity, novels and short stories. To lovers of mystery fiction, he is best known for his elegant spy-spoof *The Man Who Was Thursday*, and for his short stories starring meek, untidy Father Brown. Brown, a Catholic priest, uses a sympathy honed in the confessional to think himself into the mind of criminals, and so to solve crimes. The mysteries are simple and the stories are slight, but they live because of their gentle style, their insights into human nature, and above all for the endearing character of Father Brown himself.

The Father Brown story collections all have his name in their titles – *The Innocence of Father Brown*, *The Wisdom of Father Brown* and so on.

CHEYNEY, Peter • (1896–1951)
English writer

Cheyney wrote over 100 books, in three main series. The Lemmy Caution books (for example *Can Ladies Kill?*) are about a hardboiled, two-fisted New York 'G' man. The Slim Callaghan books (for example *The Urgent Hangman*) are about a wisecracking, dry-witted private eye working in London's club- and gangland. The 'Dark' series (all of whose titles include the word 'Dark', for example *The Stars are Dark*) are second-world-war spy stories, full of secret missions, double agents and suspenseful action.

 Read on

▶ **To the Caution books:**
  ▷Mickey Spillane, *Vengeance is Mine!*; Raymond Marshall, *Lady, Here's Your Wreath.*
▶ **To the Callaghan books:** Gordon Ashe, *The Crime Haters*; ▷P.B. Yuill, *Hazell Plays Solomon.*
▶ **To the 'Dark' books:** ▷John Creasey, *Dangerous Quest*; ▷David Dodge, *The Lights of Skaro.*

CHRISTIE, Agatha • (1890–1976)
English writer

Christie's 84 novels are models of the English 'golden age' of detective fiction. She had no mission to upgrade the genre, or to change society. Each book chronicles a crime and its solution, with total efficiency. She never wastes a word, and uses dialogue to speed her prose. Excitement mounts as we read, until none of us pauses long enough to examine each brilliantly-placed (and even more ingeniously concealed) clue. She often sets herself technical problems: in one book, the narrator is the murderer; in another, all the suspects did the crime; in another there are no survivors.

Her series detectives include Superintendant Battle, Tommy and Tuppence Beresford (who appear first in *The Secret Adversary* (1922) as 'bright young things', and finally in *Postern of Fate* (1973) as 'bright old things'), and two of the best loved and most parodied detectives in the genre, Hercule Poirot and Miss Marple. Each of these has a besetting sin, essential to the sleuthing: Poirot's confidence in his 'little grey cells' and Miss Marple's nosiness.

Poirot is at full stretch in *Murder on the Orient Express* (1934), a mystery for which he provides two entirely plausible solutions. Miss Marple uses her knowledge of people gained from gossip in the village of St Mary Mead to solve her crimes, and one of the best is *A Murder is Announced* (1950). Like a conjuror Christie shows two vital clues with one

Read on

▶ Patricia Wentworth, *The Gazebo*; Emma Page, *In Loving Memory*; Isaac Asimov, *Union Club* (short stories); Marian Babson, *Guilty Party* (a spectacular spoof).

hand, so to speak, while waving to distract our attention with the other.

Christie's Poirot books include *Murder in Mesopotamia, Appointment With Death, Mrs McGinty's Dead* and *Cat Among the Pigeons*. Her Marple books include *The Body in the Library, 4.50 From Paddington, They Do It With Mirrors* and *Sleeping Murder*. Her non-series novels include *Ten Little Niggers/Ten Little Indians/And Then There Were None, Ordeal by Innocence* and *Death Comes as the End* (set in ancient Egypt). Her 30 short-story collections include *The Labours of Hercules* and *Thirteen Clues for Miss Marple*. She also wrote plays (including *The Mousetrap* and *Witness for the Prosecution*), and (as 'Mary Westmacott') romances including *Absent in the Spring, A Daughter's a Daughter* and *The Burden*.

CHRISTMAS

▷Agatha Christie, *Hercule Poirot's Christmas/Murder for Christmas/A Holiday for Murder*
  Martha Grimes, *Jerusalem Inn*
▷Cyril Hare, *An English Murder/The Christmas Murder*
▷Georgette Heyer, *Envious Casca*
▷Michael Innes, *Christmas at Candleshoe*
▷Charlotte MacLeod, *God Rest Ye Merry*
▷Ngaio Marsh, *Tied Up in Tinsel*

CLANCY, Tom ● (born 1947)
US writer

Clancy writes blockbuster cold-war thrillers, massively exciting but depicting all Americans as kindly, home-lovin' good guys and all Russians as sinister, humourless villains. Cardboard propaganda apart, the books are crammed with dazzlingly detailed action sequences, especially the first (and best), *The Hunt for Red October* (1984), about the world's security services hunting a renegade Soviet submarine and its defecting crew. Clancy's other books are *Red Storm Rising, Patriot Games, The Cardinal of the Kremlin* and – for a change, choosing Colombian drug-barons as villains – *Clear and Present Danger*.

 Read on

▶ Nelson de Mille, *The Talbot Odyssey*; Graham Masterton, *Sacrifice*.

CLARK, Eric • (born 1937)
English writer

Clark writes action thrillers, usually with a background of espionage. Two typical books are *The Sleeper* (1979), whose hero, a Fleet Street journalist with an Eastern European background, is suddenly called into action after 30 years by his KGB controllers, and *Send in the Lions* (1981), in which five hostages (including a Hollywood film star, the Soviet Deputy Foreign Minister, and someone who seems harmless but in fact is the most important prisoner of all) are held to ransom for the release of imprisoned terrorists.

 Read on

- *Black Gambit.*
▶ Walter Wager, *Telefon*; ▷Robert Ludlum, *The Parsifal Mosaic*; Colin Dunne, *Hooligan*; Ted Willis, *The Left-Handed Sleeper.*

CLARKE, Anna • (born 1919)
South African/English writer

Clarke's novels are studies of ordinary people under psychological stress – domestic chillers. In *One of Us Must Die* (1978), for example, a woman shares her house, in increasing desperation, with her deranged husband, a disturbed teenage girl and her minister father who may not be quite as saintly as he seems. A dark secret – the mysterious death of a child 15 years before – overshadows all their lives, and the question is not whether murder will be done, but how soon and by whom to whom.

Clarke's other novels include *The Darkened Room, Legacy of Evil, Letter from the Dead* and *The Poisoned Web*.

 Read on

- *Poison Parsley.*
▶ ▷Ruth Rendell, *An Unkindness of Ravens*; ▷P.M. Hubbard, *The Quiet River*; ▷Helen McCloy, *The Slayer and the Slain*; ▷Vera Caspary, *The Man Who Loved His Wife.*

CLEARY, Jon • (born 1917)
Australian writer

Each of Cleary's suspense novels is set in a different location and tackles a different kind of problem. *The Pulse of Danger* (1966) is a chase story set in the Himalayas. *The Liberators/Mask of the Andes* (1971), about the struggle to win political rights for Bolivian peasant farmers, includes breathtaking mountaineering scenes. *Peter's Pence* (1974) is a 'caper' novel about stealing priceless works of art from the Vatican.

Cleary has also written several books starring Detective Scobie Malone of the Sydney Police. Malone is no ordinary policeman, but is called in to solve awkward and 'oddball' crimes. In *Dragons at the Party* (1987), for example, an

 Read on

▶ **To Cleary's adventure novels:** ▷Hammond Innes, *Campbell's Kingdom*; ▷Richard Condon, *Winter Kills*; Brian Moore, *The Colour of Blood.*
▶ **To the Malone novels:** June Drummond, *I Saw Him Die*; Thomas Harris, *Black Sunday*; ▷John Crosby, *Party of the Year.*

international terrorist, in league with Aboriginal activists, is trying to assassinate the President of Palucca at the Australian Bicentennial. In *Babylon South* (1989) two crimes, 20 years apart, become linked, and the investigation involves not only a super-rich Sydney business family but also Malone's own police commissioner. The books are exciting, splendidly tortuous, and full of witty comments on white Australian political and social life.

Cleary's other novels include *The Sundowners, Forests of the Night, The Fall of an Eagle, The Safe House* and *High Road to China*. His other Malone books are *The High Commissioner, Helga's Web, Ransom* and *Now And Then, Amen*. *These Small Glories* and *Pillar of Salt* are short-story collections.

CLIFFORD, Francis • (1917–75)
English writer

'Francis Clifford' was the pseudonym of Arthur Leonard Bell Thompson. He wrote action thrillers, some set in South East Asia where he worked as a young man, others set in the poorest, most troubled spots on earth (including two of his finest books, *The Blind Side* and *Amigo, Amigo*, using the backgrounds of Biafra and Central America respectively). His novels include *The Naked Runner, All Men are Lonely Now, A Wild Justice* and *Drummer in the Dark* (1976). The last is about a British intelligence officer's hunt across cold-war Europe for a treacherous, amoral drugs smuggler.

 Read on

- *The Grosvenor Square Goodbye.*
- ▷Graham Greene, *The Third Man*; ▷John le Carré, *The Little Drummer Girl*; ▷Lionel Davidson, *Making Good Again.*

COBURN, Andrew • (born 1932)
US writer

Coburn's psychological suspense novels have large casts, complex plots and build powerful climaxes slowly and inexorably. Few writers are better at the 'corrupt small town' genre, and at the twists within twists which keep you reading to the very last line. His books include *The Babysitter, Off Duty, Company Secrets, Sweetheart* and *Love Nest*. *Widow's Walk* (1984) involves a series of murders in the seaside resort of Boars' Bluff, a kind of Peyton-Place-On-Sea where police chief Paul Jenkins must use all his knowledge of local corruption and politics to solve the crimes.

 Read on

- *Goldilocks* (about a small, calm and infinitely treacherous New England town thrown into turmoil by the arrival of a beautiful, tall, blond psychopath).
- ▷Trevanian, *The Main*; ▷Vera Caspary, *A Chosen Sparrow*; Helen Nielsen, *Darkest Hour.*

COE, Tucker • (born 1933)
US novelist

Read on

'Tucker Coe' is one of the pseudonyms of ▷Donald E. Westlake. His books are private-eye novels in the tradition of ▷Chandler and ▷Ross Macdonald. They star a disgraced ex-policeman, Mitch Tobin, racked with guilt for the death of his partner. Each investigation is part of Tobin's own psychological rehabilitation, so that the stories have an ongoing psychological fascination as well as being gripping, fluent thrillers in their own right. They are best read in sequence, and are: *Kinds of Love, Kinds of Death, Murder Among Children, Wax Apple, A Jade in Aries, Don't Lie to Me.*

▶ ▷Ross Macdonald, *The Chill*; T. Jefferson Parker, *Laguna Heat*; ▷Nicolas Freeling, *Dressing of Diamond.*

COFFIN, Peter
see LATIMER, Jonathan

COLD-WAR THRILLERS

▷Ted Allbeury, *The Man With the President's Mind*
▷Tom Clancy, *The Hunt for Red October*
▷Richard Condon, *The Manchurian Candidate*
  Nelson de Mille, *The Talbot Odyssey*
▷Bryan Forbes, *A Song at Twilight*
▷Helen MacInnes, *The Venetian Affair*
  Graham Masterton, *Sacrifice*
▷Craig Thomas, *The Bear's Tears*

COLLINS, Michael • (born 1924)
US writer

Read on

'Michael Collins' is a pseudonym of Dennis Lynds, who has written mysteries of all kinds, from children's stories to Charlie Chan film scripts, under half a dozen names. As 'Michael Collins' he writes novels starring the one-armed New York private eye Dan Fortune. They are in classic style: Fortune is as wisecracking as Sam Spade, as world-weary as Philip Marlowe, as compassionate as Lew Archer. The plots begin simply, usually with a request to Fortune to find a missing person, but spiral into stories of enormous complexity and decadence, in which Fortune is the only decent

▶ ▷Hillary Waugh, *The Glenna Powers Case*; ▷Ross Thomas, *Briarpatch*; ▷Ross Macdonald, *Blue City*; ▷Ernest Tidyman, *Shaft.*

person in an amoral, corrupt world, and lays his life on the line with every step he takes. The Fortune books include *The Brass Rainbow*, *Walk a Black Wind*, *Blue Death*, *The Nightrunners*, *The Slasher* and *Freak*.

COLLINS, Wilkie • (1824–89)
English writer

Collins was a friend of Charles Dickens, and wrote the same kind of expansive, unhurried prose. His long novel *The Woman in White* (1860) is a melodrama of thwarted love and skullduggery over an inheritance, all linked by the mysterious apparition of the Woman in White herself. It falls halfway between such Victorian stories as *Wuthering Heights* and the psychological thrillers of such modern writers as ▷Barbara Vine. *The Moonstone* (1868) is a more straightforward (though not shorter) tale of intrigue, haunting and death, centred on a jewel stolen from an Eastern Buddhastatue. It is regarded as the forerunner of all modern detective novels – and also contains, in Sergeant Cuff, the first working policeman in English literature to use 'scientific' methods of investigation.

 Read on

● *The Law and the Lady.*
▶ To *The Woman in White*: Emily Brontë, *Wuthering Heights*; Charles Dickens, *Bleak House*; ▷Barbara Vine, *The House of Stairs*.
▶ To *The Moonstone*: Anna K. Green, *The Leavenworth Case*; ▷Peter Lovesey, *Wobble to Death*; ▷Freeman Wills Crofts, *The Cask*.

COMEDY THRILLERS

George Baxt, *Swing Low, Sweet Harriet*
▷Lawrence Block (or 'Chip Harrison'), *Make Out With Murder*
Leo Bruce, *Case for Three Detectives*
M. Butterworth, *Five Million Dollar Prince*
▷Stephen Dobyns, *Saratoga Headhunter*
Tony Kenrick, *Two for the Price of One*
Marion Mainwaring, *Murder in Pastiche*
Craig Rice, *Trial by Fury*
▷Donald E. Westlake, *Somebody Owes Me Money*

CONDON, Richard • (born 1915)
US writer

Condon used to work in films, and he writes in a fast-moving, step-by-step style, a written equivalent of the picture flow of film. This contrasts brilliantly with the complex

 Read on

● *Any God Will Do* (about a charming, deranged crook in pre-1914 New York, convinced that he is the unacknowledged

subjects of his books: international swindles, elaborate crimes (such as Mafia murders), conspiracies to infiltrate political systems and topple governments. If you want to know, in second-by-second detail, how to engineer the collapse of the Hong Kong Stock Exchange, plan an assassination or steal a space shuttle, Condon is the novelist to read. Many of his books (for example the 1980s trilogy *Prizzi's Honour*, *Prizzi's Family* and *Prizzi's Glory*, about an upwardly mobile Mafioso) are black farce – and the further over-the-top his plots and characters go, the more poker-faced his style. Others (for example *Mile High*, about Prohibition and *Winter Kills*, about a ruthless, Kennedy-like, US political dynasty) are hard-biting political thrillers. *The Manchurian Candidate* (1959), though its details are now somewhat dated, is the cold-war chiller to end them all.

Condon's 'caper' novels include *The Vertical Smile*, *Arigato* and *The Whisper of the Axe*. His 'straight' thrillers include *The Ecstasy Business*, *Money is Love* and *Death of a Politician*. *And Then We Moved to Rossenara* is an autobiographical book about setting up home in Ireland.

son of a European aristocrat, who embezzles a fortune and sets out for Europe to claim his inheritance).

▶ **To Condon's comedies:** ▷ Donald E. Westlake, *Cops and Robbers*; Kurt Vonnegut, *Breakfast of Champions*.

▶ **To his more serious thrillers:** Gore Vidal, *Kalki*; ▷ Patricia Highsmith, *The Talented Mr Ripley*.

▶ **To Any God Will Do:** Jerome Weidmann, *Other People's Money*; Thomas Mann, *Confessions of Felix Krull*, *The Emperor of America*.

Isaac Asimov, *Authorized Murder*
▷ H.R.F. Keating, *Death and the Visiting Firemen*
Jane Langton, *Emily Dickinson is Dead*
F. Lyall, *Death in Time*
Sharyn McCrumb, *Bimbos of the Death Sun*
Barbara Wilson, *The Dog Collar Murders*
▷ Eric Wright, *The Night the Gods Smiled*

COOK, Bob
English writer

In Cook's splendid comedy thriller *Paper Chase* (1989), four old codgers, retired intelligence agents, are goaded into writing their memoirs. They have had such humdrum careers that the stories have to be fiction, and the old men invent lurid and spectacular past lives for themselves. The British government, unable to confirm or deny the stories, bans the book, which promptly becomes a best-seller. Then

 Read on

● *Questions of Identity*.
▶ ▷ Dorothy Gilman, *The Unexpected Mrs Pollifax/Mrs Pollifax Spy*; ▷ Graham Greene, *Our Man in Havana*; Joyce Porter, *Rather a Common Sort of Crime*.

the group is approached to help in a real espionage situation involving chemical weapons, and they blunder on, applying half-forgotten maxims and attended by luck in stupendous proportions.

COURTROOM STORIES

Henry Cecil, *According to the Evidence*
▷Erle Stanley Gardner, *The Case of the Hesitant Hostess*
Anthony Gilbert, *And Death Came Too*
▷Michael Gilbert, *Blood and Judgement*
▷Margaret Millar, *Spider Webs*
Scott Turow, *Presumed Innocent*
▷Michael Underwood, *The Injudicious Judge*
▷Hillary Waugh, *Parrish for the Defence/Doctor on Trial*
▷Sara Woods, *The Law's Delay*

COXE, George Harmon • (1901–84)
US writer

Coxe wrote hundreds of short stories, and over 150 crime novels. His best known series stars Kent Murdock, a newspaper photographer whose profession gains him entry to all levels of society, but also tangles him in other people's conspiracies, divorces and murders. Coxe's books are as eventful as ▷Michael Avallone's or ▷Mickey Spillane's, but less violent – and he concentrates more on characters and backgrounds, showing us not only what was done to whom, but why. Typical Murdock books are *The Jade Venus*, *The Hidden Key*, *An Easy Way to Go* and *The Last Commandment*. An example of his non-series novels is *The Candid Impostor* (1967), in which a reporter agrees to impersonate a friend, go to Panama and collect $10,000 – at which point, all kinds of entertaining hell break loose.

 Read on

▶ Ray Owen, *The Fall Guy*;
▷Ross Thomas, *Briarpatch*;
G.J. Barrett, *Guilty, Be Damned!*.

CRAIG, Alisa
see **MacLEOD, Charlotte**

CREASEY, John • (1908–73)
English writer

Few writers have matched Creasey's productivity. In a work-

 Read on

• **To the Toff books:**
written as 'Anthony Morton', the 'Baron'

ing life of 40 years, he produced some 560 full-length novels, as well as short stories, plays and edited collections. He used 22 pseudonyms and wrote well over 20 million words. Some of his works (for example his plays, and most of his children's books) are potboilers. But three novel series, at least, are excellent.

The Toff books (written under his own name and with 'Toff' in every title) are light-hearted stories about a gentleman adventurer who sleuths for the fun of it. The Inspector West books (written under his own name and with 'West' in each title) star a Scotland Yard detective, and combine brilliant investigation (by West) with a persuasive picture of the detective's private and family life. The Gideon books (written as 'J.J. Marric' and with 'Gideon' in every title) are London police-procedurals showing Gideon and his Scotland Yard colleagues patiently working on several interlocking crimes at once. If anyone in future years wants to know what police routine was like in a mid-twentieth-century English city, these low key, documentary-style novels will give a clear picture – as well as being reliable, even engrossing fictional entertainment. (In 1990, William Vivian Butler began writing Gideon books as 'J.J. Marric': the first was Gideon's Fear.)

series (for example The Baron and the Beggar).

- **To the West books:** written as 'Jeremy York', the 'Folly' series (for example Close the Door on Murder).
- Prepare for Action (a 'Department Z' thriller, about counter-espionage during the second world war).
- ▶ **To Creasey's Toff and Baron books:** ▷Leslie Charteris, The Last Hero/The Saint Closes the Case; Barry Perowne, The A.R.P. Mystery.
- ▶ **To his West books:** Dorothy Simpson, The Night She Died; ▷Dell Shannon, Case Pending.
- ▶ **To his Gideon books:** Eric Bruton, The Laughing Policeman; ▷Lesley Egan, A Case for Appeal.

CRIMES TO COME
(crime stories and thrillers set in the future)

▷Isaac Asimov, The Caves of Steel
 Ben Bova, The Multiple Man
 Philip K. Dick, Do Androids Dream of Electric Sheep?/ Bladerunner
▷Peter Dickinson, King and Joker
▷Paul Erdman, The Last Days of America
 William Gibson, Neuromancer

CRISPIN, Edmund • (1921–78)
English writer

'Edmund Crispin' was the pseudonym of Bruce Montgomery, who was known under his own name as a composer, notably

 Read on

- Buried for Pleasure (in which Fen goes to the remotest and sleepiest

of film music for British comedies of the 1940s. His books feature one of the great 'English eccentric' detectives – Gervase Fen. Fen is a professor of English literature at Oxford, a man who 'attracts curiosities' as a flower attracts bees, a delicious amalgam of Sherlock Holmes and Jacques Tati. Crispin's plots similarly blend the intriguing, the macabre and the farcical – he is particularly good at chase endings, simultaneously unravelling knots and tying up loose ends in a scramble as hilarious as the last reel of any film comedy. Typical of his books are two Oxford University romps, *The Case of the Gilded Fly/Obsequies at Oxford* (1945) and *The Moving Toyshop* (1946).

Crispin's other novels are *Holy Disorders, Swan Song/Dead and Dumb, Love Lies Bleeding, Buried for Pleasure* (see Read On), *Frequent Hearses/Sudden Vengeance, The Long Divorce/A Noose for Her* and *The Glimpses of the Moon. Beware of the Trains* and *Fen Country* are collections of short stories.

CROFTS, Freeman Wills • (1879–1957)
English writer

Crofts' novels are masterly accounts of meticulous, plodding policework, his detective (in most books, Inspector French) unpicking tightly woven tissues of lies and alibis with painstaking, unhurried care. Many of the alibis – and hence the stories – hinge on train times: as ▷John Dickson Carr was to the locked-room mystery, so Crofts was to the timetable. The 30 French novels begin with *Inspector French's Greatest Case*, and include *Sir John Magill's Last Journey, The Mystery of the Sleeping Car Express, Death of a Train, Anything to Declare* and the particularly gripping *The 12.30 from Croydon*, in which obsession with timetables not only leads to the solution of the crime, but is what causes it in the first place.

Crofts' (excellent) non-French books include *The Cask, The Pit-Prop Syndicate* and *The Groote Park Murder*.

CROSBY, John • (born 1912)
US writer

Crosby's thrillers tell complex stories in a clear, wry style, and often centre on such huge contemporary problems as interracial tension and international terrorism. His books

of English villages to stand for parliament, and finds – as always – a crew of wildly murderous eccentrics, as if he had stumbled on the cast of an even blacker than usual Ealing comedy).

▶ ▷Michael Innes, *The Weight of the Evidence*; ▷Cyril Hare, *When the Wind Blows/The Wind Blows Death*; ▷H.R.F. Keating, *Is Skin-Deep, Is Fatal*; ▷Nicholas Blake, *The Widow's Cruise*.

 Read on

▶ ▷Cyril Hare, *Tenant for Death*; J.J. Connington, *The Sweepstake Murders*; Maurice Procter, *The Midnight Plumber*.

 Read on

• *Company of Friends* (a spy story whose main theme, unusually for the genre, is not hatred or distrust but friendship).

CROSS

include *Nightfall*, *Party of the Year*, *Dear Judgement*, *Wing-walker* and *Snake* (1983), whose background of 1960s 'flower power' and campus terrorism lets Crosby explore the interplay between crime, politics and the 'oxygen of publicity'.

AN AFFAIR OF STRANGERS (1975)
In this action-packed story of Middle Eastern terrorism, Crosby unsentimentally describes the love between Muslim Chantal and Jewish Ferenc, arouses our sympathy for both sides, and gives an absorbing account of why terrorists choose to do what they do. He deals honestly with difficult issues, and at the same time writes a magnificently gripping and eventful thriller.

CROSS, Amanda • (born 1926)
US writer

'Amanda Cross' is the pseudonym of Carolyn Heilbrun, a former Professor of English at Columbia University. Her sleuth, Kate Fansler, is also a professor, and her investigations often involve some kind of literary detection. A wry view of the place of women, both in literature and society, colours but never overwhelms the books: *A Death in the Faculty*, for example, is very funny about Harvard men's attitude to a woman professor, and about militant feminism. Cross's stories move swiftly, and yet have time for the rich, leisurely dialogue about books, music, politics and everything under the sun, which is as surely a pleasure in her work as it is in that of (say) ▷Michael Innes or ▷Edmund Crispin. Her books include *In the Last Analysis*, *The James Joyce Murder*, *Poetic Justice*, *The Theban Mysteries* and *A Question of Max*.

SWEET DEATH, KIND DEATH (1984)
Professor Patrice Umphelby, unpopular for her views on the status of women in academic life, unexpectedly kills herself. Kate Fansler investigates, drawing ideas from the suicide notes of Stevie Smith and Virginia Woolf.

CRUZ SMITH, Martin
US writer

Cruz Smith is best known for his razor-sharp thriller *Gorky Park*, set in Moscow (see below), and its sequel *Polar Star*

▷Lionel Davidson, *The Sun Chemist*; ▷John le Carré, *The Little Drummer Girl*; ▷Robert McCrum, *The Fabulous Englishman*.

 Read on

• *No Word From Winifred* (about a search for the niece of an eminent literary lady – who bears more than a passing resemblance to Mary Renault and ▷Dorothy L. Sayers).
▶ ▷Jessica Mann, *Captive Audience*; Jane Langton, *Emily Dickinson is Dead*; John Trench, *Docken Dead*.

 Read on

• *Polar Star* (in which Renko, disgraced and working as fish-gutter on a factory ship, has to

(see Read On). But he has also written reflective, ruminative novels drawing on his own Amerindian (Navajo) background. These include *The Indians Won* (1970) (set in a US of east and west coasts divided by a central Indian block) and *Nightwing* (1986) (about a Hopi deputy, brought up as a white man, exploring his alienation from both cultures as he tries to find the home of plague-carrying vampire bats).

GORKY PARK (1981)

Arkady Renko is a cynical Moscow policeman, and the novel begins as a straightforward police procedural. Gradually Cruz Smith introduces elements of the espionage thriller, and shows how the world he describes functions not by traditional notions of good and bad, but by the degrees of paranoia felt by rival security services. The setting is unusual, but it is the escalating pace and tension which make this book outstanding.

CUNNINGHAM, E.V. • (born 1914)
US writer

'E.V. Cunningham' is the pseudonym of Howard Fast (author of such historical epics as *Citizen Tom Paine*, *Spartacus* and *The Immigrants*). He wrote a series of thrillers, each with a woman's name as the title (*Sylvia*, *Phyllis*, *Penelope*, *Millie* and a dozen others). In each the heroine is an innocent plunged into bizarre and nightmarish adventures. The woman in *Sally* (1967), for example, hires someone to murder her because she thinks she is terminally ill – only to find that the diagnosis was mistaken. Cunningham's other novels star the Japanese detective Masao Masuto, who lives in Beverly Hills and solves ▷Chandlerish mysteries not by being drugged or beaten up like Philip Marlowe but by the application of gentle, Zen Buddhist methods of thought. The collision of Eastern philosophy and the materialism of Hollywood is pungently described, and the mysteries are as fascinating as the locations.

The Masuto novels include *The Case of the One-Penny Orange*, *The Case of the Russian Diplomat* and *The Case of the Poisoned Eclairs*.

find a killer and uncover a conspiracy before the ship leaves Arctic ice – or be killed himself).

▶ **To Cruz Smith's thrillers:** Fridrikh Neznansky, *The Fair at Sokolniki*; ▷Robert Moss, *Moscow Rules*.

▶ **To his Amerindian books:** ▷Tony Hillerman, *Listening Woman*; ▷Brian Garfield, *Relentless*.

 Read on

▶ **To Cunningham's thrillers:** ▷Philip MacDonald, *The Nursemaid Who Disappeared/Warrant for X*; ▷Helen McCloy, *A Change of Heart*.

▶ **To the Masuto novels:** ▷Sara Paretsky, *Killing Orders*; ▷James Melville, *A Haiku for Hanae*; Leonard Holton, *Flowers by Request*.

CUSSLER, Clive • (born 1931)
US writer

In *Raise the Titanic* (1976), Cussler's best-known action thriller, the sunken cruise-liner holds a secret. Whoever discovers that secret will rule the world – and the Americans, led by maritime troubleshooter Dirk Pitt, are racing the Russians to raise the ship from its watery grave in the icy North Atlantic. Deals, betrayals, and pounding physical action on land, in the air and below the churning sea make for a brilliantly successful recipe repeated in other Cussler blockbusters such as *Mayday!*, *Night Probe!*, *Pacific Vortex!*, *Deep Six* and *Treasure*.

 Read on

▶ Paul Gallico, *The Poseidon Adventure*; ▷Hammond Innes, *Atlantic Fury*; ▷Andrew Garve, *The Sea Monks*.

D

DAVIDSON, Lionel • (born 1922)
English writer

A sense of place and highly original ideas mark all David-son's work – and he takes his time writing each book, letting it simmer until not a word seems out of place. *The Night of Wenceslas* (1961) is about a young Englishman on the run from the secret police in Czechoslovakia. *The Rose of Tibet* (1962) is an adventure story set in Tibet just after the Chinese invasion. *Making Good Again* (1968), set in 1960s Germany, is about the aftermath of Nazism and the quest for reparations after the second world war, and *The Chelsea Murders/Murder Games* is a whodunnit set in the London art world.

Three books are set in Israel, Davidson's adopted home. *A Long Way to Shiloh/The Menorah Men* (1966) describes a hunt for the Menorah, a relic from King Solomon's Temple lost for 2000 years. *Smith's Gazelle* (1971) is about an Israeli boy and an aged Arab who join together, in the face of national politics, to try to save an almost extinct species of gazelle. The hero of *The Sun Chemist* (1976) is an Englishman researching claims that Chaim Weizmann, first president of Israel, invented a replacement fuel for petrol, made from sweet potatoes. This discovery, stifled in the 1930s by oil interests, was of enormous political importance to a modern world economically dominated by the Arab oil-producing nations.

 Read on

▶ **To Davidson's thrillers:**
▷ Geoffrey Household, *The Life and Times of Bernardo Brown*; ▷ Jon Cleary, *The Liberators/Mask of the Andes*.
▶ **To *The Chelsea Murders*:** ▷ Peter Dickinson, *Sleep and His Brother*.

DEATH IN MOSCOW

Noel Behn, *The Kremlin Letter*

DEIGHTON

▷Martin Cruz Smith, *Gorky Park*
▷Dick Francis, *Trial Run*
▷Stuart M. Kaminsky, *Black Knight in Red Square*
  Ivy Litvinov, *His Master's Voice*
▷John Trenhaile, *A Man Called Kyril*

DEIGHTON, Len • (born 1929)
English writer

In the 1960s, fired by dislike of snobbish spy fantasies of the James Bond school, Deighton produced a series of books (beginning with *The IPCRESS File*, 1962) showing spies as ordinary human beings, functionaries of a ridiculous and outdated bureaucracy in which orders for paperclips could take precedence over reducing the danger of nuclear war. Other writers have since taken up the 'spies are human' theme, but few can equal Deighton for sheer grittiness of incident or the throwaway, insolent wit of his leading characters. He has also written several documentary, 'dossier' novels (using lists, letters, memoranda, meeting-transcripts, diary entries and technical notes) on non-spy subjects. These include *Bomber* (1970), an evocation of what it was probably like to prepare for and make an RAF bombing raid in 1943, and *SS-GB* (1978), a nightmarish vision of what might have happened if Britain had lost the second world war and were now under Nazi rule.

BERLIN GAME (1982)

This book, the first of a trilogy (the other volumes are *Mexico Set* and *London Match*) is one of the most convincing novels of the 'which one of my colleagues is the double agent?' type. Bernard Samson is sent to persuade an East Berlin source, Brahms Four, to keep on working for British Intelligence – and in the process discovers that MI5 has been penetrated for years; the question is by whom? All Samson's colleagues are suspects, and are so well drawn that you don't want it to be any of them.

Deighton's other spy novels include *Funeral in Berlin*, *Horse Under Water*, *Spy Story* and another trilogy, *Hook, Line and Sinker*. *Close-up* is a black satire on the film business. *Only When I Larf* is a comedy about confidence tricksters. *Goodbye Mickey Mouse* is a 'dossier' novel about USAF personnel manning a nuclear-weapons airfield in the UK.

 Read on

- *Yesterday's Spy*; *Twinkle, Twinkle, Little Spy.*
- ▶ **To Deighton's spy-stories:** ▷John le Carré, *The Perfect Spy*; ▷Adam Hall, *The Berlin Memorandum/The Quiller Memorandum*; ▷Ted Allbeury, *The Secret Whispers*; Charles McCarry, *The Miernik Dossier.*
- ▶ **To his flying stories:** ▷Gavin Lyall, *Midnight Plus One*; Peter George, *Red Alert* (about the accidental triggering of the nuclear holocaust).

DETECTIVES IN OTHER COUNTRIES OR CULTURES

Joan Fleming, *When I Grow Rich* (Turkey)
▷Tony Hillerman, *The Blessing Way* (Amerindian: Navajo)
Timothy Holme, *The Assisi Murders* (Italy)
▷H.R.F. Keating, *Inspector Ghote Caught in Meshes* (India)
William Marshall, *The Far Away Man* (Hong Kong)
▷James McClure, *The Steam Pig* (South Africa)
▷James Melville, *A Haiku for Hanae* (Japan)
▷Maj Sjöwall and Per Wahlöö, *The Laughing Policeman* (Sweden)
▷Arthur Upfield, *The Man of Two Tribes* (Australia)
Janwillem van de Wetering, *The Streetbird* (Holland)
▷Robert van Gulik, *Judge Dee* (ancient China)

DEXTER, Colin • (born 1930)
English writer

The setting of Dexter's Inspector Morse novels is the compact, ancient English city which just happens to contain the university of Oxford. Dexter is, however, less interested in students and dons than in the way adultery, blackmail and murder nestle just under the placid-seeming bustle of ordinary Oxford life. The books centre on the relationship between cultured, moody Morse and his home-loving, unflappable assistant Sergeant Lewis. The series includes *Last Seen Wearing, The Dead of Jericho, The Wench is Dead* and *The Secret of Annexe 3* (1986). This last book begins with adultery and continues with (apparently unconnected) murder during a New Year's Eve fancy dress party at a small private hotel on the edge of town.

DICKINSON, Peter • (born 1927)
English writer

Dickinson wrote several novels starring Superintendent Pibble of Scotland Yard, a man as characterless as blotting paper. Pibble's lack of notability is vital, enabling him to blend unobtrusively with the bizarre societies in which Dickinson places the crimes: a group of New Guinea aboriginals living in the attic of a north London house (*Skin Deep/The Glass-Sided Ants' Nest*, 1968); a crazy religious community waiting for the apocalypse on a remote Scottish

 Read on

• *Service of All the Dead; The Wench is Dead.*
▶ Katharine Farrer, *Gownsman's Gallows;* S.T. Haymon, *Death and the Pregnant Virgin.*
▷Reginald Hill, *Child's Play;* ▷Sheila Radley, *Who Saw Him Die?*

 Read on

• **To the Pibble books:** *One Foot in the Grave.*
• **To *Perfect Gallows:*** *Hindsight.*
▶ **To Dickinson's larkier crime books:** ▷H.R.F. Keating, *Death and the Visiting Firemen;* ▷Andrew Taylor, *Waiting for the End of the World;*

island (*The Seals/The Sinful Stones*, 1970); a community of brain-damaged, psychically sensitive children (*Sleep and His Brother*, 1971). In later books, Dickinson abandoned Pibble but kept the bizarreness, letting the characters sort out the crimes themselves. In *King and Joker* (1976) for example, someone commits murder in a Buckingham Palace inhabited by an egalitarian, trendy-left royal family whose dark secrets give the book its fun.

Dickinson's 1980s books are less crime novels than novels including crime. Our interest is in the people and their relationships, and in Dickinson's virtuoso writing technique – he is particularly fond of moving backwards and forwards between historical periods, showing how people's behaviour today is affected by betrayals, love affairs and murders 20 or 30 years before.

PERFECT GALLOWS (1988)
The book begins stunningly, with a hanged man swinging in the dovecote of a run-down old house in the English countryside, and the odd behaviour of the young man who finds the body. As the story continues, we find out not only whodunnit, but more about the eccentric family owning the house, the GIs occupying its grounds (this is 1944), and the effect finding the corpse has on the young man, both at the time and 40 years later, at the height of his career.

Dickinson's non-Pibble novels include *A Summer in the Twenties*, *The Last House-Party*, *Death of a Unicorn*, *Tefuga* and *Skeleton in Waiting*. He has also written many prizewinning children's books, including *Tulku*, *Annerton Pit* and a science fiction trilogy, *The Devil's Children/The Changes*.

Faye Kellerman, *The Ritual Bath*.
▶ **To his novels:** ▷P.D. James, *A Taste for Death*; ▷Barbara Vine, *A Dark-Adapted Eye*; John Irving, *A Prayer for Owen Meany*.

DICKSON, Carter • (1906–77)
US writer

'Carter Dickson' was the pseudonym of ▷John Dickson Carr, whose books under his own name make excellent follow-ups. The Carter Dickson books star a large, shambling eccentric, Sir Henry Merrivale (also known as 'HM' and 'the Old Man'). Like Doctor Fell in the John Dickson Carr books, Merrivale loves food, drink and impossible mysteries. But he is far grosser than Fell, far more self-indulgent and self-delighted. The reason this series was written under a pseudonym seems to be that Carr regarded his Fell books as

 Read on

● *The Red Widow Murders.*
▶ ▷Rex Stout, *Even in the Best Families/The Best Families*; ▷Edmund Crispin, *The Case of the Gilded Fly*; ▷Anthony Morton, *The Baron and the Chinese Puzzle*; John Mortimer, *Rumpole of the Bailey*.

serious, his Merrivale books as farce. The plots are equally ingenious, however, and Merrivale, if anything, shows even greater brilliance at solving locked-room mysteries.

THE TEN TEACUPS (1937)

Ten teacups are set on a table in a house mysteriously rented only a few days before. The victim is invited to pay a visit – and so are the Metropolitan Police. When the police arrive, they find the victim dead in a locked, sealed room, with no sign of how the murderer got in or out. Chief Inspector Masters is, as always, baffled, calls in Sir Henry Merrivale, and, as always, is infuriated as much by the Old Man's brilliance at solving mysteries as by the melodramatic way he chooses to make, and to announce, his discoveries.

Dickson's two dozen 'Henry Merrivale' books include *The White Priory Murders*, *The Judas Window/The Crossbow Murder*, *My Late Wives*, *He Wouldn't Kill Patience* and *The Cavalier's Cup*. *The Department of Queer Complaints* is a collection of short stories.

DOBYNS, Stephen • (born 1941)
US writer

Dobyns' Charlie Bradshaw novels spoof every cliché of the private eye genre. Bradshaw, a wisecracking retired police-man, runs a down-at-heel detective agency in Saratoga Springs. His former boss dislikes him for his mouthiness. His contacts with the racing world mean that he constantly runs up against arrogant rich bastards and bitches with plenty to hide. Whenever murders happen – and that means frequently – Bradshaw gets the blame. Private eye spoofs are a well-worn seam, but Dobyns still mines gold.

SARATOGA HEADHUNTER (1985)

McClatchy, a crooked jockey about to give prosecution evidence against his former cronies, appears at Bradshaw's cottage late one night asking for protection. When he is found decapitated the next day, Bradshaw is the chief suspect. He has to clear his name by finding the real murderer, but every potential source of information quickly ends up dead.

 Read on

- *Saratoga Swimmer;*
  Saratoga Longshot.
- ▷Gregory Mcdonald,
  Fletch Won; ▷Lawrence
  Block, *Five Little Rich Girls;*
  Michael Allegretto,
  Death on the Rocks.

DODGE, David • (born 1910)
US writer

Dodge wrote fast-moving thrillers, notable for their intricate plots and wisecracking, tongue-in-cheek dialogue. His best known book, *To Catch a Thief* (1952, about an amateur jewel thief on the French Riviera so successful that all the professionals set out to put him or her out of business) was filmed by Hitchcock with Cary Grant – exactly the right director and star to catch the flavour of Dodge's work. There are two main series: the joky Whitney books, starring a tax accountant sucked unwillingly into investigating crime wherever he goes, and the hardboiled Colby books, starring a world-weary private eye in Mexico City. There are also half a dozen independent thrillers, usually set in Europe.

The Whitney books are *Death and Taxes, Shear the Black Sheep, Bullets for the Bridegroom* and *It Ain't Hay*. The Colby books are *The Long Escape, Plunder of the Sun* and *The Red Tassel*. Dodge's other thrillers include *The Lights of Skaro* and *Loo Loo's Legacy*. He also wrote humorous travel books, several – for example *With Knife and Fork Down the Amazon* – set in South America.

 Read on

▶ Dorothy B. Hughes, *Ride the Pink Horse*; ▷ Jonathan Latimer, *The Lady in the Morgue*; ▷ Eric Ambler, *The Mask of Dimitrios/Coffin for Dimitrios*; ▷ Robert B. Parker, *The Judas Goat*.

DOYLE, Arthur Conan • (1859–1930)
English writer

A doctor with very few patients, Doyle began writing to improve his income. His Sherlock Holmes stories were meant as potboilers, and throughout his life he claimed (while still continuing to write them) to be embarrassed by their success. The Holmes stories were published by *Strand Magazine* in the UK and by *Harper's* in the USA; these papers also serialized Doyle's Professor Challenger novels (beginning with *The Lost World*), about a flamboyant scientific genius and explorer.

THE MEMOIRS OF SHERLOCK HOLMES (1893)
In each of the 11 stories in this collection, Holmes is presented with a problem which seems insoluble – at least so far as his friend and chronicler Dr Watson can see – and solves it by a mixture of dazzling deductive reasoning and melodramatic adventure. He is particularly expert at seeing the significance of clues other people overlook – the type of mud on a person's boots, the state of someone's fingernails,

 Read on

● *The Case Book of Sherlock Holmes.*
▶ **To Doyle's Holmes stories:** Nicholas Meyer, *The Seven-Per-Cent Solution*; Richard L. Boyer, *The Giant Rat of Sumatra* (two of the most convincing of many books starring Holmes and Watson since Doyle went out of copyright); Arthur B. Reeve, *The Silent Bullet/The Black Hand*; H.F. Heard, *A Taste for Honey*; ▷ G.K. Chesterton, *The Innocence of Father Brown* (short stories).
▶ **To his Challenger books:** ▷ John Buchan,

the number of times a dog barks in the night. Doyle's single-minded, confident style perfectly suits both Holmes's character and the mysteries he is set to solve.

Doyle's Holmes novels are *A Study in Scarlet*, *The Sign of Four*, *The Hound of the Baskervilles* and *The Valley of Fear*. The short stories are collected in *Adventures of Sherlock Holmes*, *The Return of Sherlock Holmes*, *His Last Bow* and *The Casebook of Sherlock Holmes*. Apart from *The Lost World*, Doyle's Challenger books include *The Poison Belt* and *The Land of Mist*.

DRISCOLL, Peter • (born 1942)
English writer

Driscoll's thrillers – many set in South Africa – brilliantly tie up the murkier threads of politics and espionage. Although his stories are fiction, he uses real events and political movements as background. Each book racks up tension until finally it bursts out in a (vigorously described) chase to the death. Driscoll's novels include *The White Lie Assignment*, *Pangolin* (set in Hong Kong), *In Connection With Kilshaw* (set in Northern Ireland), *The Barboza Credentials*, *Heritage* and *The Wilby Conspiracy* (see below).

THE WILBY CONSPIRACY (1972)
Wilby, a black South African resistance leader, escapes to the border after the Sharpeville massacre, and although he gets through, it is obvious there has been an attempt to betray him. Many years later, one of the suspected betrayers, Shack, escapes from prison . . . The plot spirals to involve Keogh, a white mining engineer on holiday from Zambia – and to raise brooding questions about the parts played by each member of the original conspiracy, and by BOSS, the South African secret police. What game are they playing now, and why?

Prester John; Jules Verne, *Journey to the Centre of the Earth*.

 Read on

- *Spearhead* (about an attempt to free a long-imprisoned black nationalist leader).
- ▷Wessel Ebersohn, *Closed Circle*; ▷Geoffrey Jenkins, *In Harm's Way*.

DRUGS

▷Tom Clancy, *Clear and Present Danger*
▷John Crosby, *Take Two Prisoners*
▷E.V. Cunningham, *Wabash Factor*

▷Len Deighton, *Horse Under Water*
 Lesley Grant-Adamson, *Guilty Knowledge*
▷Jack Higgins, *A Season in Hell*
 Derek Lambert, *Triad*
 Elizabeth Lemarchand, *Who Goes Home?*
▷Gregory Mcdonald, *Fletch*
 Hugh McLeave, *Death Masque*
 Peter Turnbull, *Dead Knock*

DUNNETT, Dorothy • (born 1923)
Scottish writer

Dunnett is best known for two series of historical novels, the Lymond and Niccolò books. Under the name 'Dorothy Halliday', she has written a completely contrasting series, the six 'Dolly' books, and they have recently been reissued under her own name. They are light-hearted suspense novels, set in the twentieth century and all featuring Dolly, the yacht belonging to painter and master investigator Johnson Johnson. Each book has a different exotic location and a different heroine: a singer in *Dolly and the Singing Bird/The Photogenic Soprano*, a cook in *Dolly and the Cookie Bird/Murder in the Round*, an astronomer in *Dolly and the Starry Bird/Murder in Focus*, and so on. Johnson takes a hand in sorting out the incomprehensible, eventually menacing circumstances, in which each heroine is involved. The 'Dolly' books are that rare thing, romantic thrillers with brains, instead of mush, between the ears.

DOLLY AND THE BIRD OF PARADISE (1983)
Rita Geddes, a high-class makeup artist, takes a permanent job with international media personality Natalie Sheridan. On the way from the airport, someone tries to rape Rita – the start of a plot which becomes more breathless and complicated with each page, as it moves from Madeira to the Caribbean and takes in a hurricane, pirates, drug-running and a final resolution in the midst of a lava lake.

DURBRIDGE, Francis • (born 1912)
English writer

Durbridge's characters are affluent, well-connected, middle-class – and murderous. He is a master of the layer-on-layer story, and concentrates more on plot construction (at which

 Read on

• *Dolly and the Doctor Bird/Match for a Murderer*; *Dolly and the Nanny Bird*.
▶ ▷Elizabeth Peters, *Street of the Five Moons*;
 ▷Charlotte MacLeod, *The Palace Guard*; Jilly Cooper, *Prudence*.

 Read on

• *The Geneva Mystery* (Temple); *Bat Out of Hell* (non-Temple).
▶ **To Durbridge's Temple books:** ▷Anthony

he is superb) than on background. His best known books star the crime writer Paul Temple and his wife Steve. Typical are *Paul Temple Intervenes, Paul Temple and the Harkdale Robbery, The Curzon Case* and *Paul Temple and the Madison Case* (1988), which involves a luxury liner, a millionaire searching for his roots and a sinister counterfeiting gang. Durbridge's non-Temple books, usually novelizations of TV series, feature people drawn into baffling, terrifying situations. They include *The World of Tim Frazer* (and its sequels *Tim Frazer Again* and *Tim Frazer Gets the Message*), *A Game of Murder* and *Portrait of Alison* (1984), about a painter who becomes involved with diamond-smugglers.

Morton, *The Baron Goes A-Buying*; ▷ Elizabeth Ferrars, *A Murder Too Many*; ▷ Agatha Christie, *By the Pricking of My Thumbs.*
▶ **To his non-series mysteries:**
▷ Christianna Brand, *Cat and Mouse*; ▷ Michael Innes, *The New Sonia Wayward.*

E

EARLY ADVENTURE STORIES
(ancestors of the thriller)

▷ Arthur Conan Doyle, *The Lost World*
  Alexandre Dumas, *The Count of Monte Cristo*
  Jeffrey Farnol, *The Amateur Gentleman*
  H. Rider Haggard, *King Solomon's Mines*
  Anthony Hope, *The Prisoner of Zenda*
  Baroness Orczy, *The Scarlet Pimpernel*
  Stanley J. Weyman, *A Gentleman of France*

EARLY DETECTIVES
(1860s–1920s)

▷ E.C. Bentley, *Trent's Last Case/The Woman in Black* (Trent)
▷ Ernest Bramah, *Max Carrados* (Carrados)
▷ Wilkie Collins, *The Moonstone* (Sergeant Cuff)
  R. Austin Freeman, *The Red Thumb Mark* (Dr Thorndyke)
  Emile Gaboriau, *Monsieur Lecoq* (Lecoq)
  A.E.W. Mason, *The House of the Arrow* (Hanaud)
▷ Edgar Allan Poe, *Tales of Mystery and Imagination* (Dupin)
▷ S.S. Van Dine, *The Benson Murder Case* (Philo Vance)
▷ Edgar Wallace, *The Mind of Mr J.G. Reeder/The Murder Book of Mr J.G. Reeder* (Reeder)

EASTERMAN, Daniel • (born 1949)

Irish writer

Easterman's thrillers are set in magnificently described Middle Eastern and Far Eastern locations: China, Hong Kong, Iran, Saudi Arabia, Tibet. He makes real historical events the background to stories of personal bravery, loyalty and love. The books are action-packed, the characters are well-written and believable, and the exotic settings make a welcome change from the European cities favoured by so many East-West espionage thriller writers. Easterman's books are *The Last Assassin*, *The Seventh Sanctuary*, *Brotherhood of the Tomb* and *The Ninth Buddha* (1988), in which a young boy's kidnap, shortly after the first world war, sets his father on a desperate quest round India, Tibet, and the vastness of Mongolia, where White Russians and Bolsheviks are struggling to the death for political survival.

 Read on

- *The Seventh Sanctuary.*
- ▷ John Trenhaile, *The Scroll of Benevolence*; ▷ Lionel Davidson, *The Rose of Tibet*; Kenneth Benton, *Craig and the Midas Touch*; Mike Stall, *The Belshazzar Affair*.

EBERHART, M(ignon) G(ood) • (born 1899)

US writer

In the early 1930s Eberhart wrote half a dozen uninspired mystery stories starring Nurse Keate and Detective O'Leary. Several years later she began to write romantic thrillers, which were a huge success. Her novels usually centre on innocent young women who become chief murder suspects and must undertake complicated and dangerous adventures to clear their names.

 Read on

- *Speak No Evil.*
- ▷ Helen McCloy, *Through a Glass, Darkly*; Marian Babson, *The Stalking Lamb*; Phyllis Whitney, *Seven Tears for Apollo*.

NINE O'CLOCK TIDE (1978)

Who killed wealthy Sam Havlock, throwing him over a balcony to drown in the sea? Everyone suspects his pampered young wife Meade, but as the police question a houseful of guests and servants other suspicions surface, and the murderer is forced to act to evade discovery.

Eberhart's books include *Danger Money*, *Murder in Waiting*, *Woman on the Roof*, *Run Scared*, *With This Ring* and *Enemy in the House*.

EBERSOHN, Wessel • (born 1940)
South African writer

Ebersohn has written several thrillers about the viciousness of apartheid and the efforts of lone individuals (especially the white prison psychiatrist Yudel Gordon) to right particular instances of injustice. Ebersohn paints excellent pictures of violence suddenly erupting in such ordinary locations as homes, shops and schools, and his dialogue convincingly characterizes each speaker in a few blunt words. The manhunts in his books, set in wild South African scenery, are especially good. The first Gordon thriller is *A Lonely Place to Die* (1979), in which he sets out to prove the innocence of a black man charged with assassinating a white politician, and finds himself up against not only the authorities but also the local Ku Klux Klan. Later Gordon books are *Store Up the Anger*, *Divide the Night* and *Closed Circle*. *Klara's Visitors* (1987) is another kind of book entirely – a biting satire about Hitler, in the form of a diary supposedly written during his rise to power in the 1920s–30s.

Read on

- *Closed Circle.*
- ▷ *Peter Driscoll, Spearhead;* ▷ James McClure, *The Sunday Hangman;* ▷ George V. Higgins, *Outlaws.* ▷ Geoffrey Household, *Rogue Male;* Peter Niesewand, *A Member of the Club.*

EGAN, Lesley
see LININGTON, Elizabeth

EGLETON, Clive • (born 1927)
English writer

In Egleton's espionage-as-a-chess-game thrillers, your allies and colleagues may be just as much out to get you as your adversaries. The pace of his books is purposely slow, allowing a long series of small revelations to create its own hypnotic momentum, as the tapestry of deceit and treachery is stitched. He often works real news events into his plots, to good effect. Typical books are *The October Plot/The Bormann Brief*, *The Winter Touch/The Eisenhower Deception*, *A Falcon for the Hawks*, *The Russian Enigma*, *Troika*, *Death of a Sahib*, *The Triple Cross* and *A Different Drummer* (1985), which begins when files are stolen from the building housing the British Intelligence computer, and 'Dutch' Holland sets out to find out who did it – their side or our side – and why.

Egleton writes more action-packed thrillers under the pseudonyms 'John Tarrant' (*The Clauber Trigger*, *Escape to Athena*, *China Gold*) and 'Patrick Blake' (*Double Griffin*).

Read on

- *Picture of the Year.*
- ▷ Dan Sherman, *The Prince of Berlin;* ▷ Robert McCrum, *In the Secret State;* Paul Geddes, *Goliath.*

EGYPT

▷Agatha Christie, *Death On the Nile* (Poirot)
▷Agatha Christie, *Death Comes as the End* (ancient Egypt)
  A.M. Kabal, *Adversary*
▷Jessica Mann, *Death Beyond the Nile*
  Michael Pearce, *The Mamur Zapt and the Return of the Carpet*
▷Elizabeth Peters, *Curse of the Pharaohs*

ENGEL, Howard • (born 1931)
Canadian writer

Engel's private eye, Benny Cooperman, is a Jewish Canadian from Grantham, Ontario. He is shrewd, funny and soft-hearted – he must be the only sleuth ever forced to tell all by a hood threatening to remove the leaves one by one from his mother's rubber plant. The ace in his hand is that he was born and bred in Grantham, and really knows the area – both the American and Canadian sides of the border. He is no loner, and has a wry but friendly relationship with the police. But with his clients and the people he meets he can be just as much a 20-minute egg as any Spade.

A CITY CALLED JULY (1986)
Engel not only gives a good sense of place, but also does well by the seasons: summer in this case. Cooperman is hired by Jewish community leaders to investigate the disappearance of a local solicitor and his client's cash. The search sends Cooperman snooping round government contacts, mobsters and the close-knit Geller family; the plot is beautifully complex, and clues are handsomely shared with the reader (though concealed in local colour); the conclusion is brilliant.

ERDMAN, Paul • (born 1932)
US writer

A former banker, Erdman writes thrillers using his financial knowledge and his ability to predict future trends. He has a pacy style and a dry sense of humour, blending fascinating action with a resigned, world-weary view of the way greed afflicts the human race, in all nationalities and at all levels of

 Read on

- *Murder on Location; The Ransom Game.*
- ▷Robert B. Parker, *The Godwulf Manuscript*; Michael Z. Lewin, *The Enemies Within*; Peter Corris, *The Dying Trade.*

 Read on

- *The Palace* (about running a Las Vegas casino, against the odds).
- ▷Arthur Maling, *Ripoff*; William Keegan, *A Real Killing*; Jeffrey Archer, *Not*

society. His books include *The Billion Dollar Killing/The Billion Dollar Sure Thing*, *The Crash of '79* and *The Panic of '89*.

THE SILVER BEARS (1974)
Donald Luckmann is sent from California to Lugano to buy a bank. But an Iranian couple who own a silver mine, a Mafia-like organization and a ruthless financier specializing in silver futures are all cheating the bank and plotting to swindle one another. In a world where everyone is double-crossing everyone else, who will end up the winner, and who will lose?

ESTLEMAN, Loren D. • (born 1952)
US writer

Detroit is Estleman's city – and the place where his private eye, Amos Walker, works. Walker is an investigator of the old school – short of money, long on tolerance for life's losers. He is not quite as laconic as Spade or Marlowe, but is working on it. ('What happened to your face?' 'I walked into a floor'). Detroit has its quota of mean streets, and Walker gets to go down most of them. Estleman's style is an up-to-date version of the greats, and he is as good as his models at writing about eccentric or larger-than-life characters without making them seem mere freaks. His books include *Motor City Blue*, *Angel Eyes*, *The Glass Highway*, *Sugartown*, *Every Brilliant Eye*, *Yesterday* and *Any Man's Death*.

THE MIDNIGHT MAN (1983)
Walker sets out to track down a man who has killed two policemen – he wants to find him before the police arrive for a shoot-out. He meets a range of extraordinary characters, all of them dwarfed by the bounty hunter 'Bum' Bassett.

a Penny More, Not a Penny Less.

 Read on

● *Downriver.*
▶ ▷ Sara Paretsky, *Bitter Medicine*; ▷ Robert B. Parker, *Looking for Rachel Wallace*; ▷ Ross Thomas, *Briarpatch*.

F

FAIR, A.A.
see GARDNER, Erle Stanley

FALLON, Martin
see PATTERSON, Henry

FAMILIES

▷Margery Allingham, *Police at the Funeral*
  Lynn Brock, *The Kink*
▷Agatha Christie, *Taken at the Flood*
▷Peter Dickinson, *Perfect Gallows*
  Margaret Erskine, *Case With Three Husbands*
▷Henry Farrell, *What Ever Happened to Baby Jane?*
  Stephen Greenleaf, *Fatal Obsession*
▷Georgette Heyer, *Envious Casca*
▷Michael Innes, *A Change of Heir*
▷Ross Macdonald, *The Instant Enemy*
▷Ngaio Marsh, *Surfeit of Lampreys/Death of a Peer*
▷Margaret Millar, *Wall of Eyes*

FARRELL, Henry
US writer

Farrell's best known novel, *What Ever Happened to Baby Jane?* (1960), became world famous when it was filmed with Joan Crawford and Bette Davis. It is a psychological chiller about two elderly sisters, rivals all their lives (first for Daddy's love and then for fame in vaudeville and films), who pick murderously at one another's nerves, bickering to death.

 Read on

- *Death On the Sixth Day.*
- ▷Georges Simenon, *Striptease.* ▷P.M. Hubbard, *A Thirsty Evil*; Susan Hill, *I'm the King of the Castle.*

FEMALE SLEUTHS

FERRARS, Elizabeth • (born 1907)
Scottish writer

 Read on

- *Skeleton Staff.*
- ▶ Marian Babson, *There Must Be Some Mistake*; S.F.X. Dean, *By Frequent Anguish*; Joan Smith, *Masculine Ending.*

'Elizabeth Ferrars' is the pseudonym of Morna Brown. She has written over 40 psychological thrillers which take the lives of ordinary, pleasant-seeming people, and curdle them. Her style is light and easy, in marked contrast to the bizarre or horrific events she describes. She writes well about women, and is fond of close-knit communities, such as small towns (in *Alive and Dead*) or the academic world (in *Hanged Man's Noose*, in which doubt is thrown on the apparent suicide of the director of a plant research station when a mummified body is found in his house). Often, Ferrars sets her stories among a group of people who share some special interest: gourmet cookery, for example (in *Ninth Life*) or travel (in *The Wandering Widows*, set in the Inner Hebrides, and *The Small World of Murder*, set on a world cruise). Her best known books include *The Busy Body*, *The Doubly Dead*, *Last Will and Testament*, *A Murder Too Many* and *Woman Slaughter*.

A LEGAL FICTION/THE DECAYED GENTLEWOMAN (1964)

Dr Colin Lockie is surprised to be approached by Ginny, a childhood friend with whom his family have lost contact. She has located a stolen painting which once belonged to his family. Their attempts to get it back involve them with shady art-dealers and extremely unsatisfactory lawyers, and the quest is complicated for Lockie by Ginny's lies and evasions. Is she for him, against him, or varying her approach at the whim of her silly, manipulative mother?

FILTHY RICH

▷Lawrence Block, *Five Little Rich Girls*
▷Raymond Chandler, *Farewell, My Lovely*
▷Richard Condon, *The Whisper of the Axe*
  Stanley Ellin, *Very Old Money*
▷Paul Erdman, *The Billion Dollar Killing/The Billion Dollar Sure Thing*
▷Erle Stanley Gardner, *The Case of the Stuttering Bishop*
  Michael Z. Lewin, *Out of Time*
  Michael Malone, *Seasons*
▷Rex Stout, *Crime on her Hands/The Hand in the Glove*
▷Donald E. Westlake, *Jimmy the Kid*

FLEMING, Ian • (1908–64)
English writer

Fleming's James Bond books have been imitated so often that it is easy to miss how good the originals really are. Bond is a descendant of the adventure heroes of earlier writers such as H. Rider Haggard and ▷John Buchan – he wins through by a mixture of schoolboy heroics and a refusal to take himself, the world, or the villains who threaten to destroy it, seriously. In everything but plot – glossy locations, gorgeous girls, throwaway wit and splendidly over-the-top violence – the Bond films catch the exact flavour of Fleming's books.

GOLDFINGER (1959)
Auric Goldfinger has two obsessions – gold and power. He plans to smash Fort Knox with a nuclear missile and use the stolen gold to finance world domination. Only Bond can stop him – and the book shows in deadpan, second-by-second detail how he does it.

Fleming's other Bond novels are *Casino Royale/You Asked for It*, *Live and Let Die*, *Moonraker*, *Diamonds Are Forever*, *From*

 Read on

• *From Russia With Love.*
▶ ▷John Gardner, *Scorpius* (Gardner is Fleming's official successor as chronicler of Bond); Donald Hamilton, *Death of a Citizen*; Peter O'Donnell, *Modesty Blaise* (first of a series of splendidly Bondian adventures, starring the only kind of agent who could ever outsmart 007 – a woman).
▶ **More recent follow-ups:** ▷Robert Ludlum, *The Matarese Circle*; ▷Joe Poyer, *The Chinese Agenda*.

Russia With Love, Doctor No, Thunderball, The Spy Who Loved Me, On Her Majesty's Secret Service, You Only Live Twice and *The Man With the Golden Gun. For Your Eyes Only* and *Octopussy and the Living Daylights* are collections of short stories.

FLYING

▷Len Deighton, *Goodbye Mickey Mouse*
▷Dick Francis, *Rat Race*
▷Duncan Kyle, *Stalking Point*
  Brian Lecomber, *Turn Killer*
▷Gavin Lyall, *The Wrong Side of the Sky*
▷Nevil Shute, *The Rainbow and the Rose*
▷Elleston Trevor, *The Flight of the Phoenix*

FOLLETT, James
English writer

Science fiction fans know Follett for two fast-moving space thrillers – *Earthsearch* and *Earthsearch-Deathtrap*. But he mainly writes stories set in the present, often with a basis in fact. His books include: *Churchill's Gold*, set on board a US whaler hired in 1940 to replenish London bullion reserves by carrying gold from South Africa; *Mirage*, about an Israeli plot to steal blueprints of French jet fighters; and *Ice* (1978), about the global co-operation needed to deal with the situation after part of the Antarctic ice-cap breaks away, setting in train a series of events which bring the cold-war super-powers within seconds of nuclear war.

 Read on

- *Swift* (a 'caper' thriller about international computer fraud).
- ▷Geoffrey Jenkins, *In Harm's Way*; ▷Clive Cussler, *Pacific Vortex!*; ▷Craig Thomas, *Firefox*.
- **To Ice**: J.G. Ballard, *The Drowned World*.

FOLLETT, Ken ● (born 1949)
English writer

Follett's fast-action thrillers have industrial-espionage or wartime settings, and many involve real people – Churchill, for example, appears in *Storm Island/Eye of the Needle* (1978) and *The Man from St Petersburg* (1982). Follett's protagonists influence events even as the events change their lives – and he gauges the balance with great precision. *The Man from St*

 Read on

- *The Key to Rebecca* (Rommel's defeat in north Africa); *Lie Down With Lions* (set in Soviet-occupied Afghanistan); *Pillars of the Earth* (unusually, set in twelfth-century England – but just

Petersburg is about attempts to use the Russian connections of an aristocratic English family to influence events in Russia during the first world war.

STORM ISLAND/EYE OF THE NEEDLE (1978)

During the second world war, a Nazi agent finds out where the real point of the Allied attack on France in 1944 will be. The security forces discover his existence and hunt him down to stop him getting his message out. Throughout, the personalities of the agent himself, his pursuers and the family he terrorizes are sensitively drawn, and the hunt eventually reaches a nail-biting showdown on a storm-tossed island off Aberdeen.

as gripping as any of Follett's other yarns).
▶ ▷Reginald Hill, *Who Guards a Prince?*; ▷Clive Egleton, *The Russian Enigma*; George Markstein, *Soul Hunters*.

FOOD AND DRINK

Marian Babson, *Death Warmed Up*
Linda Barnes, *Cities of the Dead*
▷Elizabeth Ferrars, *Ninth Life*
Tim Heald, *Just Desserts*
▷Rex Stout, *Too Many Cooks*
L. Whitten, *Day Without Sunshine*

FORBES, Bryan • (born 1926)
English writer and film-maker

Forbes worked in British Intelligence during the second world war, and then made a successful career as film actor, writer and director. Although his thrillers are exciting, they are more concerned with the human characters and dilemmas behind real-life headlines than with sensational events. *Familiar Strangers* (1979), for example, a fictional story using the Cambridge traitors Burgess, Maclean and Philby, is a study of political loyalty and idealism in the ferment between the two world wars. *The Endless Game* (1986) begins with the murder of one inmate in an old people's home, and gradually reveals that she was not the frail innocent she seemed, but in her time had worked for MI6 in some of the most secret, most vital intelligence operations of the previous 40 years.

Forbes' other novels are *The Distant Laughter*, *The Rewrite*

 Read on

● *A Song at Twilight* (a sequel to *The Endless Game*, about a socialist Britain in the 1990s, under the thumb of the Kremlin. The main premise has been outdated by real political events, but the book is still magnificently exciting).
▶ To *Familiar Strangers*: ▷Graham Greene, *The Human Factor*; ▷John le Carré, *A Perfect Spy*; ▷Ruth Rendell, *Talking to Strange Men*.
▶ To *The Endless Game*: ▷Patrick Ruell, *Dream of Darkness*.

Man and *A Song at Twilight*. *Truth Lies Sleeping* is a collection of short stories. *International Velvet* and *The Slipper and the Rose* are novelizations of two of his film scripts, romances rather than thrillers.

▶ **To *A Song At Twilight*:**
▷ John Ball, *The First Team*.

FORBES, Colin
English writer

The strength of Forbes' action thrillers is the way he makes the geography of a place or country vital to the plot – for example Greece and Exmoor in *The Greek Key* (see Read On). His books include *The Palermo Ambush*, *The Heights of Zervos*, *The Stone Leopard*, *The Stockholm Syndicate*, *Terminal*, *Shockwave* and *Double Jeopardy* (1982). In the last, British agent Keith Martel and Swiss agent Claire Hofer team up to investigate neo-Nazis, and discover a plot to kill one of the West's leaders at a conference.

Read on

● *The Greek Key* (agents, sent to find out who is threatening to kill President Gorbachev, discover a conspiracy with its roots in Greek resistance during the second world war).
▶ ▷ Palma Harcourt, *Limited Options*; Hugh McLeave, *Under the Icefall*; ▷ Robert Ludlum, *The Parsifal Mosaic*.

FORESTER, C(ecil) S(cott) ● (1899–1966)
English writer

Forester is best known for historical adventure stories, like the 'Hornblower' series, about a British naval officer in Nelson's time. But he also wrote a classic crime novel, *Payment Deferred* (1926), which studies the psychological disintegration of an 'ordinary' man who commits murder, and a suspenseful first-world-war thriller, *Brown on Resolution* (1929). This is the story of a man captured by an enemy warship and taken to the remote island of Resolution, where he escapes and tries, single-handed, to hinder the refitting of the ship before he himself can be tracked down and killed.

Read on

● *The African Queen* (a prissy missionary and a rough-diamond ship's captain take a leaky old boat full of dynamite downriver in wartime Africa to blow up a German convoy – and fall in love on the way).
▶ **To *Payment Deferred*:**
▷ Francis Iles, *Malice Aforethought*; ▷ Georges Simenon, *The Murderer*.
▶ **To *Brown on Resolution*:**
Erskine Childers, *The Riddle of the Sands*; ▷ Geoffrey Household, *Watcher in the Shadows*.

FORSYTH, Frederick ● (born 1938)
English writer

Forsyth worked as a BBC reporter and a war correspondent, and his thrillers are as immediate and waffle-free as good

Read on

▶ Walter Wager, *Telefon*; ▷ Ted Allbeury, *The Crossing*; ▷ Daniel Easterman, *The Seventh*

news stories. They often include real people and events – only the hair-trigger tension of his plots makes actuality look tame. In *The Day of the Jackal* (1971) we follow an assassin as he stalks General de Gaulle of France. In *The Odessa File* (1972) a journalist covering the hunt for a war criminal uncovers a Nazi arms-smuggling conspiracy to help Arab terrorists in Israel. *The Dogs of War* (1974) is about a group of mercenaries seeking to topple a bloodthirsty central African dictator. In each of these books, the details are fiction, but the story is as fresh as this morning's news.

Forsyth's other novels are *The Devil's Alternative*, *The Fourth Protocol* and *The Negotiator*. *The Shepherd* is a short novel about a modern pilot in trouble given supernatural help. *The Biafra Story* is non-fiction, and *No Comebacks* is a collection of short stories.

Sanctuary; ▷ Jack Higgins, *The Eagle Has Landed*.

FRANCIS, Dick ● (born 1920)
Welsh writer

 Read on

Francis writes brilliantly paced, suspenseful thrillers. Most are about about blackmail, fraud and revenge among jockeys, owners, trainers, bookies and others involved in the racing business, though a few branch out – *Reflex*, for example, is about photography, *In the Frame* about art forgery. His books include *Dead Cert*, *Blood Sport*, *Forfeit*, *Bonecrack*, *Slay-Ride*, *Risk*, *Whip Hand*, *Proof* and *The Edge*.

- *Straight* (in which the jockey hero has to find the stolen diamonds before the bad guys find him …)
▶ John Francome and James MacGregor, *Slaughterhorse*; Grant Adamson, *Wild Justice*; Colin Dunne, *Ratcatcher*.

BREAK IN (1986)
Champion steeplechaser Kit Fielding sets out to discover why someone is trying to ruin his brother-in-law, the trainer Bobby Allardeck – and himself becomes the target of newspaper smears, bribery, entrapment and attempted murder.

FRASER, Antonia ● (born 1932)
English writer

 Read on

Jemima Shore, Fraser's TV-journalist sleuth, wears designer dresses, designer makeup, designer jewellery – and seems little more than a designer woman, a living Barbie doll. She spends her time in unusual places (a convent, a Scottish laird's castle, Oxford during the end-of-year balls), and wherever she goes murder is committed, and everyone

- *The Cavalier Case*.
▶ ▷ Dorothy Dunnett, *Dolly and the Nanny Bird*; Mary Higgins Clark, *While My Pretty One Sleeps*; ▷ P.D. James, *An Unsuitable Job for a Woman*.

hurries to tell her their innermost thoughts and motives. The stories move effortlessly along until the final chapters, when Fraser puts her brain into gear, sorts out the situation and writes a suspenseful, satisfying ending. Typical titles are *Quiet as a Nun*, *A Splash of Red*, *Cool Repentance* and *Oxford Blood*. *The Wild Island* (1978) involves Shore in dark family passions and a baroque nationalist movement in a remote highland glen, and culminates in a spectacular stalk – not for deer but for human prey.

FREELING, Nicolas ● (born 1927)
English writer

Read on

● *Not As Far As Velma.*
▶ **To Freeling's Van der Valk novels:** ▷Georges Simenon, *Maigret's Pipe*; Michael Dibdin, *Ratking*; ▷James Melville, *A Haiku for Hanae.*
▶ **To his Castang novels:** Pierre Audemars, *Now Dead is Any Man*; Mark Hebden, *Pel and the Bombers*; Roderic Jeffries, *Dead Clever.*
▶ **To his thrillers:** ▷Patricia Highsmith, *Ripley Underground*; ▷Michael Innes, *The New Sonia Wayward.*

Before Freeling began writing, he worked for 15 years as a hotel chef, all over Europe, and a strong feeling for place fills his novels. Most are police procedurals, starring the Dutch inspector Van der Valk or the French inspector Castang. Freeling's atmospheric style, full of asides and comments, lets us see his characters' reactions as they investigate, and he writes well about their home life. He has also written a number of tense thrillers, for example *A City Solitary* (1985), in which an act of petty vandalism triggers an 'ordinary, decent man' to take furious, murderous revenge.

KING OF THE RAINY COUNTRY (1965)
Jean-Claude Marschal, head of a vast secretive financial empire, disappears, and Van der Valk is assigned to find him. The trail leads Van der Valk into two kinds of unfamiliar territory: Europe's jet-set ski resorts and the seductive snares of a passionately jealous woman.

Freeling's Van der Valk books include *Love In Amsterdam*, *Because of the Cats*, *Gun Before Butter*, *Double Barrel*, *Tsing-Boum* and *Over the High Side/The Lovely Ladies*. His Castang books include *Dressing of Diamond*, *What are Bugles Blowing For?*, *Castang's City* and *Sand Castles*. His thrillers include *Valparaiso*, *This is the Castle* and *Gadget*.

FREEMANTLE, Brian ● (born 1936)
English writer

Read on

● *Charlie Muffin USA; Face Me When You Walk Away.*
▶ ▷Len Deighton, *The IPCRESS File*; ▷John le Carré, *A Small Town in*

Freemantle's books, set among spies in the cold war, are less action thrillers than psychological novels about the characters and loyalties of those employed or caught up in

Intelligence. His main hero, Charlie Muffin, is a scruffy, insubordinate non-conformist whose ordinariness makes him deeply suspect to his upper-class British superiors, but gives him a feeling of common humanity with 'lower ranks' and field operatives, including the Russians who are his official enemies. Like ▷Deighton and ▷le Carré, Freemantle shows espionage as a game, essentially foolish and pointless, but – because lives as well as loyalties are at stake – extremely dangerous. His books include *Clap Hands Here Comes Charlie/Here Comes Charlie M*, *The Inscrutable Charlie Muffin*, *The November Man*, *Goodbye to an Old Friend* and *The Run Around* (1988), in which Charlie is given the typically 'impossible' and lethal Intelligence task of locating and neutralizing a KGB assassin who has been sent to an unknown destination in Britain to murder no one knows whom.

FREMLIN, Celia ● (born 1917)
English writer

Fremlin describes the everyday lives of ordinary people – schoolgirls, shopkeepers, mothers with young children – and burns them with the acid of psychological disturbance or the supernatural. Because the surroundings are so humdrum, the menace seems all the greater, and suspense is heightened because she builds it up so gradually, page by page and chapter by chapter, to a perfectly logical, terrifying end.

THE HOURS BEFORE DAWN (1959)
Why has a schoolteacher chosen to take lodgings in Louise's house, with its harassed mother, squalling children and self-satisfied, carping husband? What is her secret – and will Louise survive the domestic pressure long enough to find out?

Fremlin's novels include *Uncle Paul*, *Seven Lean Years/Wait for the Wedding*, *Possession*, *Appointment With Yesterday*, *The Long Shadow*, *Listening in the Dusk* and *The Spider-Orchid*. *Don't Go to Sleep in the Dark* and *By Horror Haunted* are collections of short stories.

Germany; Robert Littell, *The Defection of A.J. Lewinter*.

 Read on

- *With No Crying* (about a schoolgirl who pretends pregnancy until her 'time' comes, and she must find a baby somewhere).
- ▷Margaret Yorke, *The Smooth Face of Evil*; ▷Anna Clarke, *One of Us Must Die*; Virginia Andrews, *Flowers in the Attic*.

G

GALWAY, Robert Conington

see McCUTCHAN, Philip

GARDNER, Erle Stanley ● (1889–1970)

US writer

Gardner wrote some 1000 short stories (westerns; horror; science fiction; crime), dozens of television scripts and over 150 novels. As 'A.A. Fair', he wrote 29 private-eye comic novels about the little-and-large team of Donald Lam and Bertha Cool – many of his fans rate them above all his other books. (Titles include *The Bigger They Come/Lam to the Slaughter*, *Double or Quits*, *Fools Die on Friday* and *Beware the Curves*.) Under his own name, he wrote 82 novels and dozens of short stories starring Perry Mason, a superman Los Angeles lawyer who knows how every type of character will behave in any circumstances, and exactly what question in court will instantly bring the reply he needs to win the case. Each book climaxes in a courtroom scene where Mason's brilliance completely outshines the bumbling district attorney Hamilton Burger. The books are formula hokum at its slickest – and most riveting. Recommended titles are *Th Case of the Howling Dog*, *The Case of the Curious Bride*, *Th Case of the Hesitant Hostess*, *The Case of the Footloose Doll* an(*The Case of the Careless Kitten* (1942), which (in a typicall* unlikely but compulsive Gardner twist) has Della Street Mason's own secretary, in the dock, and depends on Mason' unrivalled knowledge of cat behaviour.

GARDNER, John ● (born 1926)

English writer

Gardner is best known as ▷Ian Fleming's official successor,

Read on

▶ **To Gardner's Perry Mason books:** ▷John Dickson Carr, *Patrick Butler for the Defence*; ▷Hillary Waugh, *Parrish for the Defence*.

▶ **To 'A.A. Fair's' books:** ▷Lawrence Block, *The Burglar in the Closet*.

Read on

▶ **To the Boysie Oakes books:** ▷Brian Freemantle, *Clap Hands,*

the author of several larky and thrilling James Bond adventures. In the 1960s–70s he also wrote a series of spy spoofs starring the incompetent, slobbish Boysie Oakes (who has to hire other people to do his dirty work). His crime novels include a couple breathing life into ▷Doyle's Professor Moriarty, and his more serious spy novels include a trilogy (*The Nostradamus Traitor*, *The Garden of Weapons*, *The Quiet Dogs*) and a linked pair (*The Secret Generations*, *The Secret Houses*) combining exciting espionage plots with explorations of the way people picked up their lives (and learned to live with their wartime actions and loyalties) after the second world war.

Gardner's Bond books include *License Renewed*, *No One Lives Forever* and *Win Lose or Die*. His Boysie Oakes books include *The Liquidator*, *Amber Nine*, *Madrigal* and *A Killer for a Song*. His detective books (straightforward crime mysteries starring Inspector Derek Torry of Scotland Yard) are *A Complete State of Death* and *The Corner Men*. *Hideaway* and *The Assassination File* are collections of short stories.

Here Comes Charlie/Here Comes Charlie M; Peter O'Donnell, *Modesty Blaise*.
► **To the Torry books:** ▷Colin Dexter, *Service of All the Dead*.
► **To the serious spy novels:** ▷Len Deighton, 'Game, Set and Match' trilogy (beginning with *Berlin Game*).

GARFIELD, Brian • (born 1939)
US writer

Garfield's early books were westerns, and his later thrillers fall into a similar pattern: exciting plots, no question about who are the good guys and who the bad, little but supporting roles for women. He is best known for *Death Wish* (1973), about a New Yorker who wages a one-man vigilante campaign against muggers who have killed his wife. But his books range widely in location and time, often using real historical backgrounds. His thrillers are no-nonsense, two-fisted entertainment, models of their kind. They include *The Hit*, *Tripwire*, *Kolchak's Gold*, *Hopscotch*, *Wild Times* and *The Paladin* (1980), about a young man recruited (by Winston Churchill, no less) into British Intelligence while still at school in the 1930s, whose activities have a crucial effect on several events of the second world war.

 Read on

• *Recoil*.
► ▷Ruth Rendell, *Talking to Strange Men*; ▷Bob Langley, *Avenge the Belgrano*; ▷Eric Clark, *Black Gambit*.

GILBERT, Michael • (born 1912)
English writer

Gilbert has written television and radio plays, over 400 short

 Read on

• **To *The Crack in the Teacup*: *Sky High*.**
• **To *The Long Journey***

stories and three dozen novels of every kind, from police procedurals to adventure thrillers. He is particularly known for his novels starring Inspector Hazelrigg of Scotland Yard (they include *Close Quarters*, *Smallbone Deceased* and *Fear to Travel*), and for such breath-snatchingly exciting adventure yarns as *The Long Journey Home* (1985), about an English electronics engineer who sets out single-handed to expose a corrupt international company and finds himself at odds not only with them but with the mafia. Equally pacy is *Trouble* (1987), in which the unmasking of an IRA bombing campaign in London triggers all kinds of tensions, racial and professional, among the police and other specialists who have to deal with it.

THE CRACK IN THE TEACUP (1966)
This classic story is about a small-town solicitor who uncovers corruption involving almost every bigwig in town. In particular, who owns the Pleasuredrome, and what is its sinister connection with the Sunshine Boys' Club?

Gilbert's crime books include *Death Has Deep Roots*, *Blood and Judgement* and the short-story collections *Game Without Rules* and *Petrella at Q*. His thrillers include *The Etruscan Net*, *Flash Point* and *Paint Gold and Blood*.

Home: *The Black Seraphim*.

▶ **To Gilbert's mysteries:**
▷Cyril Hare, *Tenant for Death*; ▷Colin Watson, *The Naked Nuns/Six Nuns and a Shotgun*.

▶ **To his thrillers:**
▷George Sims, *The Last Best Friend*; ▷Duncan Kyle, *The Dancing Men*; ▷Francis Clifford, *All Men Are Lonely Now*.

GILMAN, Dorothy • (born 1923)
US writer

Although Gilman has written many children's books and eventful romantic thrillers, she is best known for her spy comedies starring Mrs Pollifax. Mrs Pollifax is an elderly lady who decides that she wants to be a spy, becomes an unofficial CIA agent, and proceeds to wreak havoc by replacing the crazy logic of so-called 'Intelligence' procedures with her own lateral thinking, based on experience of real life. The books are light, fast and funny. They begin with *The Unexpected Mrs Pollifax/Mrs Pollifax Spy* (1966), and include *The Amazing Mrs Pollifax*, *A Palm for Mrs Pollifax* and *Mrs Pollifax on Safari*.

 Read on

▶ ▷Lawrence Block, *The Cancelled Czech*; ▷Evan Hunter, *Every Little Crook and Nanny*; David Cook, *Missing Persons*.

GODEY, John • (born 1912)
US writer

'John Godey' is the pseudonym of Morton Freedgood. He

 Read on

▶ **To Godey's thrillers:**
▷Ira Levin, *A Kiss Before Dying*; ▷Jonathan

writes eventful crime thrillers, with corkscrewing, ever-surprising plots – serious capers. *The Taking of Pelham One Two Three* is about the hijack of a New York subway train. *Nella*, a brilliantly tense story of the search for a kidnapped girl, is told from a series of overlapping points of view, including that of the girl herself. In *Fatal Beauty* a mother goes to Italy to discover what has happened to her son, taken hostage by urban terrorists – and finds the situation far more complex, and more dangerous, than she imagined. Godey has also written books of a completely different kind: crime farces starring Jack Albany, an actor who is regularly mistaken for a crook – and who proceeds, each time, to play the part just for the hell of it, to see where it will lead.

Godey's other thrillers include *The Snake*, *The Talisman*, *The Fifth House* and *The Clay Assassin*. His Albany books are *Never Put Off Till Tomorrow What You Can Kill Today* and *The Reluctant Assassin/A Thrill a Minute with Jack Albany*.

Kellerman, *Over the Edge*; ▷Julian Rathbone, *Bloody Marvellous*; ▷George V. Higgins, *Outlaws*.
► **To the Albany books:** ▷Lawrence Block, *The Burglar Who Liked to Quote Kipling*; ▷Donald E.Westlake, *The Busy Body*; Les Roberts, *An Infinite Number of Monkeys*.

GOLDMAN, William • (born 1931)
US writer

Goldman is the award-winning writer of such films as *Butch Cassidy and the Sundance Kid*, *All the President's Men* and *A Bridge Too Far*. He has also written plays, non-fiction about the entertainment business, and a dozen novels. These include a terrifying thriller, *Marathon Man* (1974), later filmed with Dustin Hoffman. It is the story of a young historian who uncovers a neo-Nazi plot. The torture scene may make some readers reluctant ever to visit a dentist again, and Goldman superbly increases the suspense as his hero's quest inexorably erodes his character, destroying him psychologically.

Goldman's other novels include *Boys and Girls Together*, *Magic* and *Tinsel*, an acid Hollywood satire.

 Read on

► **To *Marathon Man*:** ▷Jonathan Kellerman, *Over the Edge*; ▷Wessel Ebersohn, *A Lonely Place to Die*.
► **To *Tinsel*:** Budd Shulberg, *What Makes Sammy Run?*.

GORES, Joe • (born 1931)
US writer

In the 1970s and 1980s Gores wrote for top-rated crime TV series, including *Kojak* and *T.J. Hooker*. He is also known for films, especially for the brooding *Hammett*, based on his novel starring the future crime writer (in his days as a

 Read on

• *Interface* (about a lone assassin, Docker, hunting down drug-dealers as they simultaneously hunt for him).

Pinkerton's agent) investigating corruption in late 1920s San Francisco. Gores has also written 100 short stories, and several novels. Three of these (*Dead Skip, Final Notice, Gone, No Forwarding*) star Dan Kearney, a car repossession agent whose work leads him into cases of corruption, mob violence and murder. Gores' non-series novels are tough crime thrillers; typical is *Come Morning* (1986), in which a jewel-thief, released from jail, sets out to track down the accomplices who put him there and at the same time to evade all the groups and individuals who hope that he will lead him to his hidden loot.

▶ **To Gores' Kearney books:** ▷Ross Thomas, *Chinaman's Chance*; ▷Gregory Mcdonald, *Fletch*.
▶ **To his non-series thrillers:** ▷Elmore Leonard, *Freaky Deaky*; ▷Richard Stark, *Point Blank/The Hunter*.

GOSLING, Paula • (born 1939)
US writer

Gosling's atmospheric crime thrillers, beginning with *A Running Duck* in 1978, rival ▷Household for excitement and ▷Rendell for psychological tension. In *A Running Duck* an assassin stalks the one woman in the country who has seen and can recognize him, and the policeman who protects her. *The Woman in Red* (1983) concerns gruesome murder among the expatriate English in Alicante, Spain. In *Monkey Puzzle* (1985) the blackmailing professor of a university English department is murdered, and in that dark, closed community things rapidly go from bad to very much worse.

Read on

● *Loser's Blues*; *The Wychford Murders*.
▶ **To *A Running Duck*:** ▷John Wainwright, *The Bastard*.
▶ **To Gosling's other books:** ▷P.D. James, *A Taste for Death*; ▷Ira Levin, *A Kiss Before Dying*; Michael Kenyon, *Zigzag*.

GOVERNMENT

▷Robert Barnard, *Political Suicide*
▷Edgar Box, *Death Before Bedtime*
▷Richard Condon, *Winter Kills*
   Robert Harling, *The Enormous Shadow*
▷Stanley Hyland, *Who Goes Hang?*
▷Duncan Kyle, *The Dancing Men*
   Edgar Lustgarten, *Game for Three Losers*
   Chris Mullins, *A Very British Coup*
   Richard Sale, *For the President's Eyes Only*
   Ted Willis, *The Left-Handed Sleeper*
   Conrad Voss Bark, *The Second Red Dragon*
   M.D. Yamani, *Beersheba Triangle*

GRAHAM, James
see PATTERSON, Henry

GRAHAM, Winston • (born 1909)
English writer

Graham is best known for historical novels set in Cornwall, especially those about the Poldark family. But he also wrote detective stories (*The Forgotten Story*, *Fortune is a Woman*, *Take My Life*) and action thrillers (*No Exit*, *Night Without Stars*, *Greek Fire*). Two of his finest books are the historical mystery *The Forgotten Story/The Wreck of the Grey Cat* (1945) and *Marnie* (1961), about a charming woman who is also a compulsive liar and embezzler, and the man who falls in love with her and tries to unlock the mystery of her character.

Graham's other books include the thrillers *The Dangerous Pawn*, *The Grove of Eagles* and *Angell, Pearl and Little God*. His mysteries include *The Riddle of John Rowe*, *The Tumbled House* and *After the Act*.

Read on

▶ **To Graham's thrillers:**
Daphne du Maurier, *The Scapegoat*; ▷Julian Rathbone, *Bloody Marvellous*.
▶ **To his mysteries:** ▷John Dickson Carr, *Fire Burn!* (historical); ▷Michael Gilbert, *The Empty House*.
▶ **To *Marnie*:** ▷Celia Fremlin, *With No Crying*.

GREAT DETECTIVES

▷John Dickson Carr, *Hag's Nook* (Gideon Fell)
▷Agatha Christie, *A Pocket Full of Rye* (Miss Marple)
▷Arthur Conan Doyle, *The Memoirs of Sherlock Holmes* (stories)
▷Gladys Mitchell, *The Twenty-Third Man* (Dame Beatrice Bradley)
▷Dorothy L. Sayers, *Murder Must Advertise* (Lord Peter Wimsey)
▷Georges Simenon, *Inquest on Bouvet* (Maigret)
▷Rex Stout, *Fer-de-Lance* (Nero Wolfe)

GREECE

▷Joan Aiken, *Last Movement*
  T.J. Binyon, *Greek Gifts*
  Margaret Doody, *Aristotle Detective*
▷Colin Forbes, *The Greek Key*

▷William Haggard, *The Heirloom*
  M.M. Kaye, *Death Walked in Cyprus*
▷Emma Lathen, *When in Greece*
▷Helen MacInnes, *Decision at Delphi*
  Helen Nielson, *Shot on Location*
▷Mary Stewart, *My Brother Michael*

GREENE, Graham • (born 1904)
English writer

Greene is known equally for 'serious', literary novels and for thrillers – or 'entertainments', as he calls them. His serious novels are psychological thrillers, showing the collapse of personality in people driven beyond control by their beliefs or circumstances. His 'entertainments' are concerned less with personality than with fast physical action.

Some are set in 1930s and 1940s Europe, and their background is the politics of the time: Nazism, Communism and jostling for influence during the years between the two world wars. *Stamboul Train/Orient Express* (1933), for example, entwines the destinies of a beautiful dancer, a lesbian reporter, a Jewish businessman, a murderer and a political revolutionary on a trans-European train journey. *The Confidential Agent* (1939) is about the representative of one party in a country wracked by civil war, trying to buy war-supplies in England, and hunted both by his political enemies and by the police.

Other 'entertainments' have more exotic locations. *The Third Man* (1950) is about the search for a sinister US drugs dealer in the rubble of Vienna just after the second world war. *Our Man in Havana* (1958) is a comedy, set in pre-Castro Cuba, about a vacuum-cleaner salesman recruited by mistake into the British Secret Service.

BRIGHTON ROCK (1938)
Pinkie, a teenage gangster in 1930s Brighton, causes the death of a seedy journalist, and is forced to marry a simple-minded waitress, Rose, to stop her testifying against him in court. As police and press close in on him, he becomes increasingly trapped in paranoia and hysteria – driven not only by the encumbering Rose or by his inept, suspicious fellow-criminals, but also by the devils of blackness and loneliness in his own soul.

Read on

• *The Ministry of Fear* (about an unremarkable, bewildered man, wandering in bomb-blasted London in 1943, tormented by the war, by outsiders who take him for a spy, and by his own guilt at having murdered his terminally sick wife).
▶ **To Greene's 'entertainments':** ▷David Dodge, *The Lights of Skaro*; ▷Geoffrey Household, *Rogue Male*; ▷Patricia Highsmith, *The Glass Cell.*
▶ **To his novels:** Paul Theroux, *The Mosquito Coast*; ▷John le Carré, *The Perfect Spy*; ▷Ruth Rendell, *A Demon in My View.*

Greene's other 'entertainments' include *It's a Battlefield* and *Loser Takes All*. His best-known novels are *The Power and the Glory*, *The Heart of the Matter*, *The Quiet American*, *The Human Factor* and *The Captain and the Enemy*. He has also written plays, travel books, an autobiography and short stories (*The Collected Stories of Graham Greene*, 1973).

H

HAGGARD, William • (born 1907)
English writer

 Read on

- *The Conspirators.*
- ▷ Anthony Price, *For the Good of the State*;
  ▷ Geoffrey Household, *Olura.*

'William Haggard' is the pseudonym of Richard Henry Michael Clayton. Most of his thrillers star Colonel Charles Russell, at first on active service with the British Security Executive, then retired. At first sight, Russell appears trapped in a view of the world which died (except in England) 70 years ago: snobbish, right-wing and contemptuous of 'little people's laws'. But he is also brave, courteous (not only to other gentlemen, but to his adversaries, to foreigners, servants and women, groups usually granted short shrift by his kind), and nobody's fool. In the same way, Haggard's books transcend right-wing fuddyduddiness by imaginative plotting and adroit characterization. The violence is brisk and bloody, and Haggard convincingly depicts a kind of moral stratosphere far above ordinary people's lives, in which the real work of managing the affairs of state is done, and in which politicians figure only as small-minded, posturing irritants.

THE HEIRLOOM (1983)
On his retirement from the Brethren (an Italian-based criminal group), George Trevisan wants to make a financial settlement with his detested Greek wife Yola, leave her and live in peace in Italy. But Yola wants more and uses her high-powered Greek contacts to try to get her Trevisan's considerable property on Corfu. Trevisan asks his friend Charles Russell to house-sit – and as a result Russell has to cope with violence, terrorism, and near-war between Greece and Italy.

Haggard's Russell books include *The Unquiet Sleep, The Vendettists, The Powder Barrel, The Old Masters/The Notch on the Knife, The Scorpion's Tale, Visa to Limbo* and *The Expatriates.*

HALL, Adam
see TREVOR, Elleston

HALLIDAY, Dorothy
see DUNNETT, Dorothy

HAMILTON, Patrick • (1904–62)
English writer

Well known as a playwright (*Rope, Gaslight*), Hamilton is also remembered for the novel *Hangover Square* (1941), a study of the mental disintegration of a man destroyed by his sordid surroundings (the mean backstreets of London) and by his love for a worthless woman. It is clinical, chilling and hypnotic.

Hamilton also wrote non-crime novels, and a trilogy (*The West Pier, Mr Stimpson and Mr Gorse, Unknown Assailant*) about a criminal mastermind, which foreshadows ▷Highsmith's Ripley books.

HAMMETT, Dashiell • (1894–1961)
US writer

Hammett wrote (originally as 'Peter Collinson') for the crime magazine *Black Mask*. His stories are in the standard style: one short sentence to a paragraph – literally 'one-liners'. The plots twist and turn, and the violence count is high. In his novels, Hammett uses similar ideas as the framework for subtler work. His detectives are wisecracking but sensitive, tough but vulnerable, involved in the mess of human affairs but aloof, as detached from their work as surgeons. His books are brilliantly plotted, exciting to read, and leave a sombre aftertaste. The first two, *Red Harvest* (1929) and *The Dain Curse* (1929), are about an unnamed Chicago sleuth, the 'Continental Op'. *The Maltese Falcon* (1930) stars Sam Spade (played in the later film by Humphrey Bogart) and *The Glass Key* (1931) features Ned Beaumont, not a sleuth but an ordinary man who risks his life to help a friend. *The Thin*

 Read on

▶ **To *Hangover Square*:**
  ▷Georges Simenon, *Act of Passion*; ▷Ruth Rendell, *A Demon in My View*.

 Read on

▶ ▷Raymond Chandler, *The Lady in the Lake*; Max Byrd, *Finders Weepers*; ▷Andrew Bergman, *The Big Kiss-off of 1944*; ▷Loren D. Estleman, *Motor City Blue*; ▷Sara Paretsky, *Indemnity Only*.

Man (1934), later the inspiration of a film series with William Powell and Myrna Loy, stars the only married, happy sleuths Hammett ever wrote about, Nick and Nora Charles.

Hammett's story-collections include *The Big Knockover/Blood Money* (Continental Op), *The Adventures of Sam Spade and Other Stories/They Can Only Hang You Once*, and *A Man Named Thin and Other Stories*.

HAMMOND, Ralph
see INNES, Hammond

HANSEN, Joseph ● (born 1923)
US writer

David Brandstetter, the hero of crime novels by Hansen, is an insurance claims investigator, no superhero but a decent, ordinary man. He is homosexual, and his work is often among the Californian gay community. Hansen's emotional observation is sharp – he is excellent, for example, on Brandstetter's edginess every time his partner, Doug, is attracted to another man. But Hansen is not writing 'gay fiction' or tracts on minority rights. In stripped, clipped prose, he offers intriguing mysteries with clearly-drawn characters and a fine sense of place. The Brandstetter books include *Fadeout*, *Death Claims*, *Troublemaker*, *Skinflick* and *The Man Everybody Was Afraid Of* (1978), in which Brandstetter travels to sleepy upcoast La Caleta to investigate the murder of Ben Orton, the all-powerful local police chief, whose family think that he was killed by gay activist Cliff Kerlee.

Read on

▶ ▷ Ross Macdonald, *The Way Some People Die*; William Campbell Gault, *County Kill*; ▷ David Dodge, *Shear the Black Sheep*.

HARCOURT, Palma
English writer

Harcourt worked for British Intelligence in several parts of the world, and uses her knowledge of foreign places to good effect. Her thrillers usually involve superpower machinations which are complicated by the private lives of the diplomats taking part. She is careful to show her characters in shades of grey, rather than all good or all bad, and often works against our expectations: a promising politician is shown to be anti-Semitic, for example, and a governess working for terrorists loves children. Harcourt's books include *A Fair Exchange*,

Read on

▶ ▷ Helen MacInnes, *Prelude to Terror*; Catherine Gaskin, *The File on Devlin*; ▷ David Dodge, *Angel's Ransom*; ▷ Colin Forbes, *Double Jeopardy*.

Dance for Diplomats, *The Twisted Tree*, *A Matter of Conscience* and *Limited Options* (1987), in which a diplomat's son is kidnapped by terrorists, who then force the boy's father to help smuggle an assassin out of France.

HARE, Cyril • (1900–58)
English writer

Alfred Gordon Clark, a County Court judge, wrote nine 'classic' detective stories under the pseudonym 'Cyril Hare'. His books are the work of a cool, drily witty legal mind, and many star the barrister Francis Pettigrew, an unassuming man whose career has never fulfilled its youthful promise. Although Hare's plots are scrupulously fair, and his glimpses of the English legal system are fascinating, it is the details of character and location which give his books their zest. *Tragedy at Law* (1942), Hare's own favourite, is a wonderful character study of Pettigrew himself – charming, gentlemanly, rueful about his lost potential. The setting of *With a Bare Bodkin* (1946) is the offices of a London ministry during the second world war. A subsidiary strand of *When the Wind Blows/The Wind Blows Death* is Hare's impression of what it is like to make and enjoy classical music. *An English Murder/The Christmas Murder* is a 'big old house' book, in which murder in a snowbound mansion is investigated not by Pettigrew but by the eccentric Czech refugee Dr Bottwink.

WHEN THE WIND BLOWS/THE WIND BLOWS DEATH (1949)

The murder in this book is that of Lucy Carless, professional soloist at a concert to be given by a small-town amateur orchestra. Pettigrew investigates – a task made difficult and distasteful by the web of guilty secrets and seething relationships which lie under the smooth façade of the society's committee meetings and its music-making.

Hare's other Pettigrew books are *That Yew Tree's Shade/Death Walks the Woods* and *He Should Have Died Hereafter/An Untimely Death*. Another detective, Inspector Mallett of Scotland Yard, appears alone in three books (*Tenant for Death*, *Death is No Sportsman* and *Suicide Excepted*), and also 'walks on' in several of the Pettigrew books.

 Read on

- *An English Murder/The Christmas Murder*.
- ▷ Michael Gilbert, *Sky High*; ▷ Michael Innes, *Hamlet, Revenge!*; ▷ Georgette Heyer, *Envious Casca*; ▷ John Sherwood, *Groves of Evil*.

HARLING, Robert • (born 1910)
English writer

 Read on

Harling's six books, part thriller part 'literary' novel, are set in the world of journalism. His interests are the ethics and motives of his characters, and the way journalists interact both with each other and with the politicians and others whose doings they report. His books include *The Endless Colonnade*, *The Hollow Sunday*, *The Athenian Widow* and *The Enormous Shadow* (1955), written just after the spies Burgess and MacLean defected to the USSR, and with a story centring on whether or not a particular politician is a traitor. Although some political and journalistic details of Harling's books have now been superceded, his work still lives for the way he evokes 1950s London, for his beautifully-crafted plots and for his characters, drawn with a journalist's eye for fascinating, revealing detail.

- *The Dark Saviour* (in which a journalist's profile of a Caribbean politician has political and social consequences far beyond his intentions).
- ▶ **From the same period:** J.M. Mallalieu, *No Love for Johnny.*
- ▶ **More modern books on similar themes:** ▷ Robert McCrum, *In the Secret State*; ▷ Bryan Forbes, *Familiar Strangers.*

HARRISON, Chip
see **BLOCK, Lawrence**

HAVING A WONDERFUL CRIME
(murderous holidays)

  Marian Babson, *A Trail of Ashes*
▷ Agatha Christie, *A Caribbean Mystery*
▷ John Creasey, *The Toff at Butlins*
▷ Elizabeth Ferrars, *The Small World of Murder*
▷ Gladys Mitchell, *The Twenty-Third Man*
▷ Gwen Moffat, *Last Chance Country*
▷ Joyce Porter, *The Package Included Murder*
▷ Mary Stewart, *The Moonspinners*

HEYER, Georgette • (1902–74)
English writer

 **Read on**

Best known for Regency romances, Heyer also wrote detective novels, notable for their humour (especially in fast-moving dialogue), bizarre characters and atmosphere, and above all for crafty, guileful plots, reminiscent of ▷ Marsh at

- ▶ ▷ Agatha Christie, *Sparkling Cyanide/Remembered Death*; ▷ Michael Innes, *Hamlet, Revenge!*; ▷ Robert Barnard, *A*

her most exuberant. Her main detectives are Superintendent Hannasyde (whose character is to have no character at all) and the go-ahead, endlessly self-confident Inspector Hemingway. She loves all the standard 'classic' ingredients: old country houses, suspicion-riven villages, festering families, poison-phials, locked rooms, daggers in the back at dead of night. Her books include *Death in the Stocks*, *They Found Him Dead*, *Envious Casca* and *Detection Unlimited*.

Corpse in a Gilded Cage; ▷Ngaio Marsh, *Spinsters in Jeopardy/The Bride of Death.*

HIGGINS, George V(incent) • (born 1939)
US writer

 Read on

Higgins worked as a lawyer, and for several years was the Massachusetts assistant district attorney. He uses the crime-novel formula as the basis for long, densely-plotted novels about the state of the USA in the late twentieth century, and is particularly concerned with the downside – drugs, poverty, racism and moral bankruptcy. Although his books take some getting into, the power of his writing (especially his descriptions of violence and his court scenes), his brilliant dialogue, and the urgency of his view that the success of the USA traps and destroys its own citizens, sweep the reader along – his thrillers are exciting, but they also make you think.

• *Wonderful Years, Wonderful Years.*
▶ John Gregory Dunne, *True Confessions*; E. Richard Johnson, *Silver Street*; Don de Lillo, *White Heat.*

OUTLAWS (1987)
The book begins with a robbery committed by a gang of student dropouts in 1970. There is no apparent motive, but in the following years, as the gang's crimes increase in ferocity, we see that their actions arise from disgust with the 'American way of life' – and the Boston establishment, symbol of all that they have rejected, begins to take slow but sure revenge.

Higgins' other novels include *The Friends of Eddie Coyle* and its sequel *The Digger's Game*, *Cogan's Trade*, *A City on a Hill*, *The Rat on Fire*, *A Choice of Enemies*, *Impostors* and *Trust*. *The Sins of the Fathers* is a short-story collection.

HIGGINS, Jack • (born 1929)
English writer

 Read on

'Jack Higgins' is the pseudonym of ▷Henry Patterson. Patterson published under several names until the success of

• *Storm Warning.*
▶ ▷Frederick Forsyth, *The Day of the Jackal;*

HIGHER EDUCATION

The Eagle Has Landed (see below) in 1975, after which he concentrated on the Higgins name, and republished many of his earlier books as Higgins. His books are adventure thrillers, often set in wartime, and are pacy, violent and full of character. The 'Jack Higgins' books include *The Last Place God Made, A Prayer for the Dying, The Eagle Has Landed, Hell is Always Today, The Dark Side of the Street, Solo, Cold Harbour* and *A Season in Hell* (1989), about a young ex-SAS officer taking revenge on drug barons who have killed two apparently harmless young addicts.

THE EAGLE HAS LANDED (1975)

During the second world war, a group of German commandos parachutes into a quiet Norfolk village to assassinate Churchill, who is staying there for the weekend. Compared to most war thrillers, in which the only difference between enemy soldiers and cardboard targets is that the enemy bleed when shot, this novel depicts the Germans as believable human beings – something which greatly enhances the power of Higgins' already gripping tale.

Alexander Fullerton, *Regenesis*; Gerald Seymour, *Kingfisher*.

HIGHER EDUCATION

Catherine Aird, *Parting Breath*
▷Edward Candy, *Words for Murder, Perhaps*
▷Amanda Cross, *A Death in the Faculty*
S.F.X. Dean, *By Frequent Anguish*
Charlotte Epstein, *Murder in China*
▷Elizabeth Ferrars, *A Murder Too Many*
David Gethin, *Dane's Testament*
▷Paula Gosling, *Monkey Puzzle*
▷Reginald Hill, *An Advancement of Learning*
▷Michael Innes, *The Weight of the Evidence*
▷P.D. James, *Shroud for a Nightingale*
▷Jessica Mann, *Captive Audience*
▷Josephine Tey, *Miss Pym Disposes*

HIGHSMITH, Patricia • (born 1921)
US writer

Except for *Edith's Diary* (1977, about a woman frantically

 Read on

• *The Two Faces of January*
(about a young man,

trying to cope with a mentally deficient son and a senile uncle after her husband leaves her) and *The People Who Knock on the Door* (1982, about the disintegration of an 'ordinary' American family whose father becomes a born-again Christian) Highsmith's books are all psychological thrillers. Many – notably the four Ripley books (about a charming psychopath) – show the progress of horribly convincing, 'everyday' murders, and the way killing erodes the murderer's moral identity. In others, a simple, innocent action or decision is like the first step up a ladder – each rung leading to something more terrifying than the one before, and which is gradually being pulled away from the characters as they climb. Few writers screw tension so tight in such functional, unemotional prose.

FOUND IN THE STREET (1986)

In New York, paranoia capital of the world, Jack Sutherland lives a creative, happy life – until he loses his wallet in the street. Linderman, a compulsive do-gooder, finds it and returns it. From that moment every character in the book – Linderman, Jack, Jack's wife and child, and above all the innocent, beautiful Elsie – are trapped in a spiral of tension and bewilderment which leads gradually but inescapably to murder.

Highsmith's Ripley books are *The Talented Mr Ripley*, *Ripley's Game*, *Ripley Under Ground* and *The Boy Who Followed Ripley*. Her other novels include *Strangers on a Train*, *The Glass Cell*, *The Story Teller/A Suspension of Mercy*, *The Tremor of Forgery* and *This Sweet Sickness*. She has published seven collections of short stories: *Eleven*, *The Animal-Lover's Book of Beastly Murder*, *Little Tales of Misogyny*, *Slowly, Slowly in the Wind*, *The Black House*, *Mermaids on the Golf Course* and *Tales of Natural and Unnatural Catastrophes*.

HILL, Reginald • (born 1936)
English writer

Hill writes two kinds of books. Under his own name, he writes crime novels starring Superintendent Dalziel and Sergeant (later Inspector) Pascoe. Under his own name, and as 'Dick Morland' and 'Patrick Ruell', he writes adventure and psychological thrillers. The heart of the Dalziel and Pascoe books is the relationship between canny, slobbish Dalziel and university-educated, fastidious Pascoe. The

psychologically disabled by his love for his puritanical, unloving father, who thinks he sees the old man in the street, follows him, and finds himself attached to a criminal as a fly is attached to the spider which sucks it dry).
► Julian Symons, *The Man Who Killed Himself*; Joseph Hayes, *The Desperate Hours*; ▷Georges Simenon, *The Hatter's Ghosts*; ▷Celia Fremlin, *Appointment With Yesterday*.

 Read on

• To *Child's Play*: *Deadheads* (about Patrick Alderman, whose amazing good luck at work and in life seems always to be connected with people's death. He is a keen rose-grower – is

settings for each crime are often congenial to one of the partners but not to the other (for example a rugby club in *A Clubbable Woman*, and a teacher training college in *An Advancement of Learning*). This puts pressure on a relationship which is already strained and strengthened by dissimilarities. Books in the series include *Ruling Passion, An April Shroud, Bones and Silence* and *A Pinch of Snuff*.

Typical of Hill's fast-moving, absorbing thrillers are *The Long Kill* (which begins when a hired assassin falls in love with the daughter of his intended victim), and *Who Guards a Prince?* (1982), in which the determination of both families to stop the marriage between an Irish-American girl and an English royal prince spirals into kidnapping, murder and the uncovering of an international conspiracy of Freemasons. A typical Ruell thriller is *Dream of Darkness*, the portrait of a teenager disturbed by memories of the atrocities she saw in Amin's Uganda as a child.

CHILD'S PLAY (1987)
When rich Gwendoline Huby dies, her relatives' hopes run high. So do those of other people: an animal charity, representatives of the local civic theatre and a fascist political group. All are disappointed, and some are insulted. The atmosphere grows ever more poisonous, until someone is murdered, and Dalziel and Pascoe are called in to investigate.

HILLERMAN, Tony • (born 1925)
US writer

Hillerman began writing detective novels in the 1970s, as a way (he says) of showing people Amerindian (Navajo) ways, customs and traditions. His detectives (Lieutenant Joe Leaphorn and Sergeant Jim Chee) work in the Navajo reservation, and their cases usually involve some interaction between Amerindians and white people, or depend for solution on knowledge of some Navajo legend or pattern of thought. Hillerman's plots are exciting, his style is clear and his Amerindian lore is fascinating without making the books seem preachy or over-exotic. Typical titles are *The Blessing Way, Talking God, People of Darkness, A Thief of Time* and *Listening Woman* (1978), in which investigation of a linked pair of murders takes Leaphorn physically into the desert fringes of the reservation, and psychically into the souls of a

he deadheading other people to suit himself?)

● **To *Who Guards a Prince?*:** *A Very Good Hater*.

▶ **To Hill's Dalziel and Pascoe books:** Pat Flower, *Fiend of the Family*; ▷ Sheila Radley, *The Chief Inspector's Daughter*; ▷ Colin Dexter, *The Silent World of Nicholas Quinn*.

▶ **To his non-series novels:** ▷ Duncan Kyle, *The Dancing Men*.

▶ **To Ruell's psychological novels:** ▷ Winston Graham, *Marnie*; ▷ Patricia Highsmith, *Ripley Under Ground*.

 Read on

● *Dance Hall of the Dead; The Dark Wind*.

▶ ▷ Martin Cruz Smith, *Nightwing*; ▷ Brian Garfield, *Relentless*; ▷ Peter Dickinson, *Skin Deep/The Glass Sided Ants' Nest*.

hippie student and the revenge-seekers of the Nuñi people whose gods have been profaned.

HILTON, John Buxton • (born 1921)
English writer

Hilton's books are set in the hills and villages of Derbyshire, one of the most secretive and beautiful of all English counties. His unfussy, smoothly-flowing prose contrasts with the extraordinary stories he tells, making good use of superstition, folk customs and above all the brooding menace of the area. His Brunt books (*Rescue from the Rose*, *Gamekeeper's Gallows*, *Dead Nettle*) star the Victorian/ Edwardian detective Sergeant Brunt, and are beautifully evocative of the period. His Kenworthy books star a contemporary detective whose cases involve knowledge not only of the countryside but of past local crimes and scandals. The Kenworthy books include *Death in Midwinter*, *Hangman's Tide*, *No Birds Sang*, *Some Run Crooked* and *The Anathema Stone*.

 Read on

▶ **To Hilton's Brunt books:**
▷ Arthur Conan Doyle, *The Hound of the Baskervilles*; Francis Selwyn, *Sergeant Verity and the Imperial Diamond*.
▶ **To his Kenworthy books:** ▷ Roy Lewis, *Witness My Death*; Lionel Black, *Breakaway*; ▷ Michael Gilbert, *The Empty House*.

HIMES, Chester • (1909–84)
US writer

Himes worked in France and originally wrote in French, publishing non-crime novels before making his name with the Harlem series. His nine Harlem novels, starring Coffin Ed Johnson and Grave Digger Jones, tell of knifings, rapes and drug-pushing in the realistic-seeming slums and grimy streets of Harlem. But letting Johnson and Jones solve the crimes is the last thing on Himes's mind. He is describing a nightmare, a surrealist ghetto filled with grotesque, unlikely characters. His real subjects are black identity in a white society, and the way evil seethes like lava just below the surface of slum life, just needing the smallest vent-hole to erupt. Like ▷ Chandler, Himes wrote in a sharp, one-liner-packed style of his own, moving his books even further from reality. On the surface they read like pacy, funny, violent crime stories – underneath they cut like knives.

The Johnson and Jones books are *For Love of Imabelle/A Rage in Harlem*, *The Crazy Kill*, *The Real Cool Killers*, *All Shot Up*, *The Big Gold Dream*, *Cotton Comes to Harlem*, *The Heat's On/Come Back Charleston Blue* and *Blind Man With a*

 Read on

▶ **New York crime novels in a similar sharp, tough style:** ▷ Ed McBain, *Ax*; ▷ Joseph Wambaugh, *The Glitter Dome*.
▶ **Non-crime novels sharing Himes's vision of Harlem:** James Baldwin, *Go Tell it on the Mountain* and *Another Country*.

HOUSEHOLD

Pistol/Hot Day, Hot Night. Harlem crime novels with other heroes are *Run Man Run* and *Une Affaire de viole* (*A Case of Rape*). Himes' non-crime novels include *If He Hollers Let Him Go*, *Cast the First Stone* and *Pinktoes*.

HOUSEHOLD, Geoffrey • (1900–88)
English writer

Many of Household's books are 'chase' thrillers, like those of ▷Buchan, pitting single individuals against the might of sinister corporations, political groups or dastardly foreigners. His heroes are usually hunted men, forced to 'hole up' either in seedy urban lodgings or in the countryside, where they live by commando survival skills. The stiff-upper-lip, old-school-tie thriller is a favourite English form, and Household adds modern psychological edginess to it, producing a blend of physical and nervous tension which few other writers match.

ROGUE MALE (1939)
The narrator, an upper-class Englishman, has tried and failed to assassinate Hitler, has been tortured by the Gestapo, tossed over a cliff to die – and survived. Now he has to track down and unmask pro-Nazi conspirators in England, before they find him and finish him off. He spends much of the second half of the book literally 'gone to ground': hiding in an underground burrow while his enemies gather for the kill outside.

Household's thrillers include *The High Place*, *A Rough Shoot*, *A Time to Kill*, *The Courtesy of Death*, *Hostage: London* and *The Last Two Weeks of Georges Rivac*.

 Read on

- *Watcher in the Shadows.*
- ▷ ▷William Haggard, *Closed Circuit*;
  ▷Graham Greene, *A Gun for Sale/This Gun for Hire*;
  ▷Winston Graham, *Cameo*; Ivan Ruff, *Blood Country*; ▷Duncan Kyle, *The Semonov Impulse.*

HOUSES

▷Robert Bloch, *Psycho*
Elizabeth George, *Payment Deferred*
Tim Heald, *Blue Blood Will Out*
Elizabeth Lemarchand, *Change for the Worse*
Nancy Livingstone, *Trouble at Aquitaine*
▷Peter Lovesey, *Bertie and the Seven Bodies*

Holly Roth, *Crimson in the Purple*
▷Andrew Taylor, *Waiting for the End of the World*
▷Barbara Vine, *The House of Stairs*

HUBBARD, P(hilip) M(aitland) • (1910–80)

English writer

Hubbard wrote well-crafted, unsettling novels of suspense, in which small hints of menace in ordinary people and places gradually escalate to obsession, (sometimes supernatural) terror and violence. His books include *A Hive of Glass, Cold Waters, Dancing Man, The Graveyard* and *The Quiet River* (1978), in which a woman and her husband rent a house beside a fast-running, deep river which – they soon discover – is reputed to need a blood-sacrifice every two years to keep it from flooding. In the year of their move, the next sacrifice falls due . . .

 Read on

- *The Holm Oaks; A Thirsty Evil.*
- ▷Joan Aiken, *Died on a Rainy Sunday*; ▷Ruth Rendell, *Judgement in Stone*; ▷Celia Fremlin, *The Long Shadow*; Susan Hill, *I'm the King of the Castle.*

HUNTER, Evan • (born 1926)

US writer

Hunter has written pulp thrillers under several pseudonyms including 'Richard Marsten' (*The Spiked Heel, Vanishing Ladies, Big Man*). Under his own name he has published short stories, and a dozen crime novels including the gritty *The Blackboard Jungle* and *Buddwing* annd the comedy-caper *Every Little Crook and Nanny*. But he is best known for his books written as 'Ed McBain'. There are two main series. The 87th Precinct books are police procedurals set in an imaginary city not unlike New York. The books star various members of the precinct, and as the series proceeds the characters (especially McBain's main hero, Steve Carella) grow and develop, so that we come to know them like members of a family. Several books include an arch-villain, the Deaf Man, who has a macabre sense of humour not unlike the Joker in the Batman comics. The blend of humour and harshness, social comment and fantasy in the 87th Precinct books has been imitated in many TV police series, most notably *Hill Street Blues*. McBain's second series stars the Florida attorney/detective Matthew Hope, and each novel is named after a famous fairy tale, whose story gives hints and clues to McBain's plot.

McBain's 87th Precinct books (over 50 in all) include *Cop*

 Read on

▶ **To McBain's 87th Precinct books:** MacKinlay Kantor, *Signal Thirty-Two*; ▷Joseph Wambaugh, *The Choirboys*; Peter Turnbull, *Deep and Crisp and Even* (set in Glasgow).

▶ **To his Matthew Hope books:** ▷Gregory Mcdonald, *Fletch*; ▷John D. MacDonald, *One Fearful Yellow Eye.*

Hater, *Let's Hear it for the Deaf Man, Ax, Doll, Shotgun* and the particularly larky *Fuzz*. There are also several 87th Precinct omnibuses, of which the third has an especially good selection of novels. The Matthew Hope books include *Goldilocks, Rumpelstiltskin, Puss in Boots* and *Beauty and the Beast*.

HYLAND, Stanley • (born 1917)
English writer

Hyland's three detective novels, written in the 1960s, are classics of the English golden age. Their plots are devious, their backgrounds are unusual (the 'corridors of power', the Parliament building and the offices of the British civil service), and their tone is joky and irreverent. His books blend the rigorous clue-placing of a ▷Dorothy L. Sayers with the larkiness of Ealing comedy films. Their titles are *Who Goes Hang?, Green Grow the Tresses-O* and *Top Bloody Secret*.

Read on

▶ ▷Edmund Crispin, *Holy Disorders*; ▷Michael Innes, *The Weight of the Evidence*.

ICY WASTES

▷J.R.L. Anderson, *Death in a High Latitude*
▷Clive Cussler, *Iceberg*
▷James Follett, *Ice*
▷Hammond Innes, *Maddon's Rock/Gale Warning*
▷Geoffrey Jenkins, *Southtrap*
▷Duncan Kyle, *Whiteout*
▷Gavin Lyall, *The Most Dangerous Game*
▷Alistair MacLean, *Ice Station Zebra*
▷Joe Poyer, *Killer*

ILES, Francis • (1893–1971)
English writer

'Francis Iles' was a pseudonym of Anthony Berkeley Cox, who also wrote as ▷'Anthony Berkeley'. Under the name Iles, he published a handful of short stories, and three of the most highly regarded novels in the genre. They pioneered the psychological crime story, showing the deterioration of minds under intolerable stress or delusion, and the inexorable progress of crimes whose perpetrators and motives we know from the start of the book. Later writers in this vein (for example ▷Ira Levin or ▷Ruth Rendell) concentrate on creepiness. Iles blends it with sharp social criticism of the 1930s upwardly mobile: snobbery is the corrosive force which destroys his people's lives.

MALICE AFORETHOUGHT (1931)
Bickleigh, a small-town doctor, has married 'above him', and his wife never lets him forget the fact. His unhappiness leads him first to flirting with pretty women, then to a love affair,

 Read on

● *Before the Fact*; *As For the Woman*.
▶ ▷Anthony Berkeley, *Trial and Error*; Nina Bawden, *The Odd Flamingo*; ▷Patricia Highsmith, *Found in the Street*.

then to murder. He thinks that he is committing the perfect crime, and he is wrong.

INNES, Hammond • (born 1913)
English writer

Many of Innes' action thrillers are set in the services, mining, oil-drilling or seafaring. He prefers to use backdrops not of cities but of wide open spaces – oceans, mountains, deserts – and his characters usually battle the elements as well as one another. This reflects one of his major interests – the balance between human beings and the natural environment. His books include *Wreckers Must Breathe/Trapped*, *The Blue Ice*, *Maddon's Rock/Gale Warning*, *Campbell's Kingdom*, *The Mary Deare/The Wreck of the Mary Deare*, *Atlantic Fury*, *Solomon's Seal* and *Medusa* (1989), about a British skipper whose lone task it is to counteract revolution on the island of Minorca and stop the Russians establishing a strategically vital deep-water harbour in the Mediterranean. The problem is that the revolutionaries have captured the girl he loves . . .

 Read on

- *Levkas Man*. Innes also writes thrillers under the name 'Ralph Hammond' (*Isle of Strangers/Island of Peril*; *Saracen's Gold/Cruise of Danger*).
- ▷ Desmond Bagley, *Bahama Crisis*; ▷ Clive Cussler, *Pacific Vortex!*; Stephen Coulter, *Offshore!*; ▷ Geoffrey Jenkins, *Scend of the Sea*.

INNES, Michael • (born 1906)
English writer

'Michael Innes' is the pseudonym of the Oxford don J.I.M. Stewart. His 50 detective novels (starring Appleby or Honeybath) are typical of the type known as 'dons' delight': set in the unhurried world of Oxford colleges and English country houses, aglow with fine port, old-master paintings and the sound of endless, erudite quotations – which everyone, from detective to potboy, from rural yokel to damsel in distress – seems immediately able to recognize. Privilege and farce go hand in hand, in an unhurried, dazzling charade. At its worst (in, say, *The Journeying Boy*, 1949), Innes' style can now seem affected and dated. But at his best (in *The Daffodil Affair*, 1942, or *Private View/Murder is an Art*, 1952), few 'classic' detective writers so effortlessly combine mystification, urbanity and grotesquerie.

 Read on

- *The Daffodil Affair*; *A Family Affair*.
- ▷ Edmund Crispin, *The Moving Toyshop*; Glyn Daniel, *The Cambridge Murders*; ▷ Amanda Cross, *In the Last Analysis*.

OPERATION PAX/PAPER THUNDERBOLT (1951)
In a private clinic in the quiet Oxford countryside something extremely sinister – brainwashing? conditioning by drugs? plotting world domination? – is going on. A petty criminal, kidnapped by the experimenters as a human guinea pig,

escapes and hides in Oxford, where the action at once involves East European refugees, eccentric dons, the pupils of a school for especially brainy boys, and Appleby's pretty young sister Jane. The investigation climaxes in the 'stack' of the Bodleian Library, a pile of eight million books in a cavernous vault under Radcliffe Square.

Innes' crime novels include *Death at the President's Lodging*, *Lament for a Maker*, *Appleby on Ararat*, *The Weight of the Evidence*, *A Night of Errors* and *Stop Press/The Spider Strikes*. He also wrote serious novels under his own name; they include a quintet of books about Oxford life: *The Gaudy*, *Young Patullo*, *A Memorial Service*, *The Madonna of the Astrolabe* and *Full Term*.

ITALY

Oliver Banks, *The Caravaggio Obsession*
Sarah Caudwell, *Thus Was Adonis Murdered*
▷Jon Cleary, *Peter's Pence*
▷Bob Cook, *Questions of Identity*
▷Reginald Hill, *Another Death in Venice*
Timothy Holme, *The Devil and the Dolce Vita*
▷Robert Ludlum (or 'Michael Shepherd'), *The Road to Gandolfo*
▷Helen MacInnes, *North from Rome*
Sheila Moody, *Penny Royal*
▷Magdalen Nabb, *Marshal and the Murderer*
J. O'Hagan, *Death and a Madonna*
▷Elizabeth Peters, *The Seventh Sinner*

J

JAMES, P(hyllis) D(orothy) • (born 1920)
English writer

Although James was once hailed as ▷Agatha Christie's heir, she is more like a cross between ▷Sayers and ▷Highsmith. The crimes in her books are brutal, committed by deranged, psychopathic people, and are described in chilling, unblinking prose, as objective as a forensic report. She has two detectives. Chief Inspector Adam Dalgliesh is a poet and aesthete, combining brilliant detective instincts with a liberal conscience, scrupulous and tolerant in his dealings with other people. Cordelia Gray is a young woman who inherits a down-at-heel detective agency, and shows a hitherto unexpected flair for investigation and psychological perception. Although James' books at first seem long and leisurely, tension mounts inexorably until the climax – not a cosy Christieish explanation round the library fire, but a scene of pathological, cathartic violence.

A TASTE FOR DEATH (1986)
A lonely spinster, taking flowers to decorate her local church, finds the corpses of a tramp, Harry Mack, and a prominent Tory MP, Sir Paul Berowne, with their throats cut. Berowne has been the subject of recent slanderous accusations, and Dalgliesh's investigation must begin by deciding whether he was murdered or committed suicide after killing Mack. The story gradually sucks in various members of Berowne's large and mutually hostile family, his servants and his mistress – and as well as showing us this, and describing the police work in exact, unhurried detail, the book also concerns itself with the lives and preoccupations of Dalgliesh's assistants, especially Inspector Kate Miskin, the newest member of the team.

 Read on

- *The Skull Beneath the Skin* (in which Gray investigates murder on an island, committed during rehearsals for the play *The Duchess of Malfi*. Tense atmosphere, furiously exciting climax).
- ▷Ngaio Marsh, *Surfeit of Lampreys/Death of a Peer*; ▷Margery Allingham, *The Tiger in the Smoke*; ▷Patricia Highsmith, *Ripley Under Ground*; ▷Ruth Rendell, *A Sleeping Life*; ▷Margaret Millar, *Mermaid*.

James' other novels include *Cover Her Face, A Mind to Murder, Shroud for a Nightingale, An Unsuitable Job for a Woman, The Black Tower, Death of an Expert Witness* and *Devices and Desires*.

JENKINS, Geoffrey
English writer

Jenkins writes action thrillers set in hard conditions – the Antarctic (*A Grue of Ice*), the deserts of South Africa (*In Harm's Way*), the South Atlantic Ocean (*Scend of the Sea*). His heroes are hard, lonely men caught up in physically gruelling adventures. Several novels use past events as the framework for skilfully-woven modern drama.

IN HARM'S WAY (1986)
Kepler West has invented a synthetic rock which will safely hold nuclear waste. Its raw materials can be found only in the South African desert, near the site of Donald Campbell's old speed trials. Members of the International Atomic Agency are invited there to inspect the new process, and China sends a group of terrorist mercenaries to sabotage the proceedings. To complicate matters further, West falls in love with Rencha, a former terrorist. The story pelts along, and Jenkins describes the physical surroundings so that they seem to assume a character of their own, vital to the story.

 Read on

- *A Twist of Sand.*
- ▷Hammond Innes, *The Doomed Oasis*;
  ▷Duncan Kyle, *Whiteout*;
  ▷Desmond Bagley, *Running Blind.*

JUNK BONDS
(followers and imitators of 007)

▷Lawrence Block, *The Cancelled Czech*
Desmond Cory, *Height of Day/Dead Men Alive*
▷John Gardner, *The Liquidator*
Donald Hamilton, *Date With Darkness*
Peter O'Donnell, *Modesty Blaise*
▷Mickey Spillane, *Day of the Guns*

K

KAMINSKY, Stuart M. • (born 1934)
US writer

Kaminsky is best known for a series of thrillers starring Toby Peters, a 1940s private eye sacked from his previous job as film studio security guard for cheeking Jack Warner. He still works in Hollywood, and his speciality is investigating blackmail and murder involving film stars. The stars themselves take part in the investigations, and the supporting casts include such luminaries as Babe Ruth, Joe Louis and Ernest Hemingway. For all their wisecracks, the books are serious crime novels, crammed with nuggets of gossip and movie history which will delight film buffs without alienating readers who care nothing for Hollywood's great past. Typical Peters books are *High Midnight* (featuring Gary Cooper), *Bullet for a Star* (co-featuring Errol Flynn, Sydney Greenstreet and Peter Lorre) and *Murder on the Yellow Brick Road* (featuring Judy Garland).

 Read on

▶ ▷ Andrew Bergman, *Hollywood and Levine*;
▷ Jonathan Latimer, *Black is the Fashion for Dying/The Mink-Lined Shroud*.

KATZENBACH, John
US writer

Katzenbach's *The Traveller* (1987) is a terrifying psychological crime thriller, about a serial killer who keeps a young woman 'slave' to write down each gruesome detail of the way he humiliates and kills his victims. It is written with pace, tension and a remorseless eye for detail – Katzenbach's early life as a crime reporter stands him in good stead. The book's only drawback is that it describes, with lipsmacking explicitness, horrific sadism to women. If you can stomach this, you may find it unputdownable.

 Read on

• *In the Heat of the Summer*.
▶ Thomas Harris, *The Silence of the Lambs*;
▷ Jonathan Kellerman, *Blood Test*; ▷ John Wainwright, *The Bastard*.

KAVANAGH, Dan • (born 1946)
English writer

'Dan Kavanagh' is the pseudonym of Julian Barnes, known for such 'literary' novels as *Flaubert's Parrot* and *History of the World in 10½ Chapters*. The Kavanagh books star Duffy, a London policeman framed and drummed out of the force, who now runs a down-at-heel security agency. Duffy is hard-boiled and ruthless, moving easily in the worlds of London porn-merchants (*Duffy*), crooked airport baggage-handlers (*Fiddle City*), soccer-hooligan gangs (*Putting the Boot In*) and the well-heeled heels at a dodgy country mansion (*Going to the Dogs*). Kavanagh's pace is furious, his satire bites, and his descriptions of both sex and violence are as explicit as you can write this side of prosecution.

KEATING, H(enry) R(eymond) F(itzwalter)
• (born 1926)
English writer

Keating is a leading reviewer and commentator on detective fiction. In the early 1960s he wrote half a dozen brilliant spoofs, each involving murder in a different, bizarre location: at a firefighters' conference (*Death and the Visiting Firemen*), at a residential course in Zen Buddhism (*Zen There Was Murder*), at a croquet championship (*A Rush on the Ultimate*), backstage at the opera (*Death of a Fat God*). In 1965, with *The Perfect Murder*, he began a series starring Ganesh Ghote, a mild-mannered Bombay police inspector. The Ghote books (most of which have 'Ghote' in the title) are no-tricks mysteries given an exotic gloss by Keating's feeling for the sights, smells, sounds and eccentric characters of India, and by his tongue-in-cheek use of Indian turns of speech in English. Ghote is a delightful hero: fussy, self-important, easily embarrassed, proud of his home and fond of his wife, and above all wide-eyed with astonishment at the worlds his investigations plunge him into. The series is not as larky as Keating's earlier books, but it is magnificently consistent – each new book is as good, and as fresh, as all the rest.

Keating's Ghote books include *Inspector Ghote Plays a Joker* (in which Ghote tracks down a practical joker – who is immediately murdered), *Inspector Ghote Goes by Train* (a splendid variant of the 'locked-room' mystery), *Inspector*

 Read on

▶ ▷John Milne, *Shadow Play*; ▷Andrew Taylor, *Waiting for the End of the World*; ▷Stephen Dobyns, *Saratoga Headhunter*; ▷Tucker Coe, *Wax Apple*.

Read on

▶ **To Keating's early, non-Ghote books:**
▷Pamela Branch, *Murder Every Monday*; Peter Anthony, *The Woman in the Wardrobe*; ▷Donald E. Westlake, *Brothers Keepers*.

▶ **To the Ghote series:**
▷James Melville, *Sayonara Sweet Amaryllis*; Josef Skvorecky, *The Mournful Demeanour of Lieutenant Boruvka*; ▷Ellis Peters, *Mourning Raga*.

Ghote Caught in Meshes (which plunges Ghote into the mad world of Indian politics), *Filmi, Filmi, Inspector Ghote* (set in a Bombay film studio) and *The Body in the Billiard Room* (set in a stuffy British club in Poona). Keating's other crime novels include *The Dog It Was That Died* and *Is Skin-Deep, Is Fatal*.

KELLERMAN, Jonathan • (born 1949)
US writer

Like his hero Alex Delaware, Kellerman is a professional psychologist, and his compulsive, chilling thrillers depend on unlocking the secrets in apparently demented minds. In *When the Bough Breaks/Shrunken Heads* (1985), for example, Delaware is working with a disturbed seven-year-old girl who may have witnessed a bloody murder, and uncovers a story of pederasty, child prostitution and murder. In *Over the Edge* (1987) a disturbed young man is the chief suspect in a case of multiple knife-murders, and Delaware must turn every stone in wealthy Los Angeles society to prove the boy's innocence. Kellerman's themes are grim and his books are long, but his writing is mesmeric – to begin each novel is to guarantee reading it through to the shattering, surprising end.

 Read on

• *Blood Test.*
▶ ▷Sara Paretsky, *Bitter Medicine*; ▷Robert B. Parker, *Looking for Rachel Wallace*; Stephen King, *Pet Sematary*.

KEMELMAN, Harry • (born 1908)
US writer

David Small is a small-town Massachusetts rabbi, mild-mannered, easy-going, and a touch too progressive for some members of his community. Wherever he goes, murders seem to happen, threatening the suburban tranquillity. Small solves them, worrying away at the problems in the way scholars puzzle at problems in the Talmud. The books are drily witty, the mysteries beautifully worked out, and Kemelman is famous for the insight he gives into ordinary US small-town life. Not since ▷Chesterton's Father Brown stories has anyone so successfully mixed religious exposition and murderous intrigue.

 Read on

▶ Joseph Telushkin, *The Final Analysis of Doctor Stark*; Leonard Holton, *Out of the Depths*; ▷Ellis Peters, *One Corpse Too Many*; ▷E.V. Cunningham, *The Case of the Poisoned Eclairs.*

The Small books are *Friday the Rabbi Slept Late, Saturday the Rabbi Went Hungry, Sunday the Rabbi Stayed Home, Monday the Rabbi Took Off, Tuesday the Rabbi Saw Red, Wednesday the Rabbi Got Wet* and *Thursday the Rabbi Walked Out. The Nine Mile Walk* is a collection of stories of a quite different kind, about a Mycroft-Holmesian figure who sits in his study solving cases by sheer brainpower.

KINGS, QUEENS, PRESIDENTS

Jeffrey Archer, *Shall We Tell the President?*
W.F. Buckley, *Saving the Queen*
Don de Lillo, *Libra*
▷Peter Dickinson, *King and Joker*
▷Antonia Fraser, *Your Royal Hostage*
▷Reginald Hill, *Who Guards a Prince?*
▷Gavin Lyall, *The Crocus List*
Eleanor Roosevelt, *Murder and the First Lady*
R. Serling, *Air Force One is Haunted*
Margaret Truman, *Murder in the White House*

KYLE, Duncan • (born 1930)
English writer

'Duncan Kyle' is the pseudonym of John Broxholme. Some of his books were first published under the name 'James Meldrum', but have been reissued under his current pseudonym. He writes action thrillers. Some belong to the one-man-in-harsh-environment-and-deadly-danger type – enjoyable examples are *Whiteout* (a snow-and-ice survival drama) and *Terror's Cradle*, in which a journalist, following clues left by his girlfriend, is harried by both the CIA and KGB, as she possesses knowledge on microfilm that could change the world. Other Kyle thrillers (for example *The Dancing Men*) are stories of international investigation and intrigue.

THE DANCING MEN (1985)
Genealogist Warwick Todd is hired to find the personal history of a nineteenth-century Irish immigrant to the USA. His subject turns out to have been the grandfather of John Leyden, a prospective presidential candidate – and the more facts Todd unearths (travelling round the world in the course of his investigations), the more other people try to stop him in his tracks.

 Read on

● *The Honey Ant* (about the deadly games which result from the discovery of a seam of precious stones on the edge of the Great Sandy Desert in Australia).
▶ **To Kyle's 'man-against-the-elements' books:** ▷Hammond Innes, *Campbell's Kingdom*; ▷Geoffrey Jenkins, *In Harm's Way*
▶ **To his international thrillers:** ▷Reginald Hill, *Who Guards a Prince?*; ▷Colin Forbes, *Shockwave*.

L

LANGLEY, Bob • (born 1938)
English writer

Langley writes action thrillers, like a modern-day ▷Buchan. Some make real events their starting-points: the 1980s Falklands War in *Conquistadores* (1985); the 1890s British campaign in the Sudan in *The Churchill Diamonds* (1986). Langley is interested in character, particularly in the interaction of people, allies and adversaries under stress. He is also unusual in that one of his villains, Martin Segundo, appears in several books, including *Conquistadores* and *Avenge the Belgrano* (1988), which begins when a group of Argentinian commandos is sent to Scotland to fit mines to H.M.S. Conqueror, the ship which sank the General Belgrano during the Falklands War. The tensions between them, and the final chase in the Cairngorms during a snowstorm, form the story.

 Read on

- *Autumn Tiger; Traverse of the Gods* (a second-world-war story with a mountaineering theme, climaxing on the North Face of the Eiger).
▶ ▷Ken Follett, *Storm Island/Eye of the Needle*; ▷Trevanian, *The Eiger Sanction*; ▷Duncan Kyle, *Stalking Point*.

LATHEN, Emma
US writer

'Emma Lathen' is the pseudonym of Mary J. Latis and Martha Hennisart, who also write as 'R. B. Dominic'. Their 'Lathen' books combine big business, finance and murder. *Banking on Death* (1961), for example, is woven from three strands: industrial research and marketing, family trust funds and a missing heir. The mayhem in *Accounting for Murder* (1964) starts with the attempt to trace fraudulent computer accounts. *Double, Double, Oil and Trouble* (1979) deals with oil contracts, ransoms and Swiss bank accounts. In each book Lathen's investigator, John Putnam Thatcher of Wall Street's Sloan Guaranty Trust, comes hard up against the greed, naiveté and bad manners of the human race, without ever being surprised by what he finds or condemn-

 Read on

- *When in Greece.*
▶ ▷Arthur Maling, *Schroeder's Game*; ▷Paul Erdman, *The Crash of '79*; ▷David Dodge, *Loo Loo's Legacy*.

ing it. The banking and financial details are easy to understand, the characters are entertaining, and the stories move effortlessly to pounding climaxes.

As 'R.B. Dominic', the same authors write mysteries which are solved by US congressman Ben Safford. These have the same structure, with Safford's family and colleagues appearing in each, but deal with wider issues: fraudulent doctors, for example (*The Attending Physician*, 1980), political corruption (*Epitaph for a Lobbyist*, 1974), security and aircraft research (*A Flaw in the System*, 1983).

SOMETHING IN THE AIR (1988)
One of the best things about 'Lathen' is that after two dozen books she shows no sign of staleness. *Something in the Air* sets her usual lively characters to work in Sparrow Flyways, a small commuter airline. The plight of a share-holding workforce whose dwindling profits are needed for investment as well as to pay wages, the hardening arteries of a once go-ahead company, and the murderous reactions of a blackmail victim, are all grist to her mill. The Sloan Guaranty Trust is a trustee of some of the shares – and so Thatcher, urbane as ever, picks his way delicately and inexorably towards the truth.

LATIMER, Jonathan • (1906–83)
US writer

Latimer was a Hollywood screenwriter in the 1940s and 1950s, and in the 1960s scripted the Perry Mason television series. His 1930s comedy thrillers, starring the boozy private eye Bill Crane, are among the most suspenseful and funniest in the genre. In the 1950s he wrote two non-Crane books, one of which (*Black is the Fashion for Dying/The Mink-Lined Shroud*) is a murder mystery set in Hollywood.

Latimer's Crane books include *Murder in the Madhouse*, *The Lady in the Morgue* and *Red Gardenias/Some Dames are Deadly*. His other non-Crane thrillers are *Solomon's Vineyard/The Fifth Grave*, *Sinners and Shrouds* and *Dark Memory*.

 Read on

▶ Peter Coffin (Latimer himself, under a pseudonym), *The Search for My Great Uncle's Head*; ▷ Dashiell Hammett, *The Thin Man*; ▷ H.R.F. Keating, *Death of a Fat God*.

LATIN AMERICA

Bruce Buckingham, *Three Bad Nights*
W.F. Buckley, *See You Later, Alligator*
▷Jon Cleary, *The Liberators/Mask of the Andes*
▷David Dodge, *Plunder of the Sun*
▷Clive Egleton, *The Russian Enigma*
Robert L. Fish, *The Fugitive*
▷Graham Greene, *Our Man in Havana*
▷Bob Langley, *Conquistadores*
▷Alistair MacLean, *River of Death*
▷Philip McCutchan, *Werewolf*
▷Gregory Mcdonald, *Carioca Fletch*
M. Muller, *Legend of the Slain Soldiers*

le CARRÉ, John ● (born 1931)
English writer

'John le Carré' is the pseudonym of David Cornwell. He
began his career with two urbane detective stories, *Call for
the Dead* (1961) and *A Murder of Quality* (1962). He has also
written several 'literary' novels, exploring the moral dilemmas of a successful businessman (*The Naive and Sentimental
Lover*), a young terrorist (*The Little Drummer Girl*), a spy (*The
Perfect Spy*) and a boozy publisher trapped into espionage in
the early days of glasnost (*The Russia House*, 1989). But he is
chiefly known for complex, house-of-mirrors spy stories.
Unlike writers of the ▷Fleming school, who showed
espionage as a swashbuckling, Robin Hood activity with
clear rules and absolute moral standards, le Carré shows
spies as secretive, unremarkable men, morally hesitant and
trapped by their profession. Betrayal, not adventure, is their
stock-in-trade; they work in a world of remorseless moral
erosion, and le Carré chillingly shows how it functions
entirely for itself, inward-looking and self-perpetuating, with
minimal relevance to real life.

THE QUEST FOR KARLA (1974–80)
This trilogy (*Tinker Tailor Soldier Spy*, *The Honourable
Schoolboy* and *Smiley's People*) is about the British Intelligence 'circus', and especially the part played in it by a
senior official, George Smiley. Smiley's task is to investigate
double agents, 'moles', inside the service, while safeguard-
ing his own position and keeping warily in touch with

 Read on

● *The Perfect Spy.*
▶ **To the spy stories:**
▷Len Deighton, *Berlin
Game*; ▷Dan Sherman,
The Prince of Berlin; John
Lear, *Death in Leningrad*;
Julian Semyonov, *Tass is
Authorized to Announce*
(a cold-war spy-story
seen from the Russian
side).
▶ **To *The Little Drummer
Girl*:** ▷John Crosby, *An
Affair of Strangers*;
▷Doris Lessing, *The Good
Terrorist.*

contacts and rivals in the Eastern bloc. His enquiries uncover treacheries and compromises extending back over two generations.

Le Carré's other spy books are *The Spy Who Came in from the Cold*, *The Looking Glass War* and *A Small Town in Germany*.

LEGAL EAGLES

Sarah Caudwell, *Thus Was Adonis Murdered*
▷Carter Dickson, *Night at the Mocking Widow*
▷Lesley Egan, *Against the Evidence*
Anthony Gilbert, *Murder by Experts*
▷Cyril Hare, *Tragedy at Law*
Simon Michael, *The Cut Throat*
William D. Tapply, *Dead Meat*
▷Michael Underwood, *The Unprofessional Spy*
▷Sara Woods, *Bloody Instructions*

LEONARD, Elmore • (born 1925)
US writer

Until Leonard became a full-time writer in 1967, he worked in advertising, and his prose is as pacy and straight-to-the-point as that would suggest. He has written westerns, but is best known for edgy, witty crime thrillers with plot twists and blood-hammering suspense on every page. His books include: *Glitz*, *52 Pick-up*, *Unknown Man No. 89*, *Bandits*, *The Switch*, *Touch* (1987), centring on a mysterious man in downtown Detroit who 'bleeds from five wounds', heals people and works miracles, and *Freaky Deaky* (1988), about a couple of old friends, an ex-urban terrorist and an explosives expert, who join up to settle a few old scores . . .

 Read on

- *Killshot* (a compulsive 'chase' thriller about two hoodlums who set out to stalk, and kill, a couple who have accidentally seen them commit a crime).
- ▷Jonathan Kellerman, *Over the Edge*; ▷Richard Stark, *Slayground*; Colin Dunne, *Ratcatcher*.

LEVIN, Ira • (born 1929)
US writer

Levin is known for plays (including the hit comedy *Deathtrap*), for two supernatural novels (*Rosemary's Baby* and *The Stepford Wives*), and for a thriller based on the real-life hunt for the Nazi war-criminal Josef Mengele, *The Boys from*

 Read on

- Mary Carter Roberts, *Little Brother Fate*; ▷Patricia Highsmith, *Ripley's Game*; ▷Patrick Hamilton, *The West Pier*;

Brazil. His only crime novel, *A Kiss Before Dying* (1953), is often ranked as one of the best in the genre. Its 'hero' is a cold-blooded killer, murdering to win an inheritance, and although we follow his crimes in chilling detail, we are not told his identity until just before the novel's climax in a giant copper-smelting works. He could be any one of the charming, plausible young men in the story, a fact which confuses Levin's female characters, just as it confuses the reader – except that the female characters end up dead.

▷Georges Simenon, *Sunday*.

LEWIS, Roy • (born 1933)
Welsh writer

Lewis' heroes are Arnold Landon, a planning officer with an interest in historic buildings, the solicitor Eric Ward and the country policeman Inspector Crow. The mysteries in the novels are straightforward, but the books are given depth by Lewis' fascination with obscure points of law (he is the author of over twenty textbooks on land and company law), with the rugged countryside of Wales and northern England, and with such medieval crafts and skills as stonemasonry or archery. His novels are deliberately understated and unsensational; a placid treat.

Lewis's Landon books include *A Trout in the Milk, A Gathering of Ghosts* and *Men of Subtle Craft*. His Ward novels include *Premium on Death, A Limited Vision, A Certain Blindness* and *A Necessary Dealing*. His Crow books include *Error of Judgement, A Question of Degree* and *Nothing but Foxes*. His other books include *A Distant Banner, A Fool for a Client* and *A Wolf by the Ears*.

 Read on

▶ ▷Cyril Hare, *With a Bare Bodkin*; ▷Colin Dexter, *Service of All the Dead*; Lesley Grant-Adamson, *Threatening Eye*.

LININGTON, Elizabeth • (born 1921)
US writer

Linington has written historical novels, Gothic romances, and some 50 detective stories in four series, all set in the Los Angeles area. The crime series make excellent follow-ups for each other. As 'Anne Blaisdell' in the UK (and under her own name in the USA) Linington writes police procedurals starring moody Welsh-American Sergeant Ivor Maddox and his colleagues. Her police procedurals written as 'Dell Shannon' star independently-wealthy Mexican-American Lieutenant Luis Mendoza and his colleagues. As 'Lesley

Read on

▶ **US police procedurals:** Joseph Harrington, *The Last Known Address*; Rex Burns, *The Alvarez Journal*.
▶ **UK police procedurals:** ▷John Creasey, *Policeman's Dread*; Dorothy Simpson, *The Night She Died*.

Egan' she writes police procedurals starring Italian-American detective Vic Varallo, and amateur investigations starring the quiet lawyer and student of the paranormal Jesse Falkenstein.

In the police procedural books, the detectives are shown working on several cases simultaneously, clearing some up immediately and watching others twist and turn throughout the story. Linington also describes her main characters' families (including pets) and their private lives, developing them from story to story in the manner of soap opera. (Mendoza's cats, for example, especially whisky-drinking El Señor, make regular appearances.) Domestic concerns – buying houses, shopping, love affairs, pregnancy – give the books interest outside the mystery, and there are sometimes clues and hints in the 'family' scenes which set the detectives on useful new tracks.

The Maddox books (by Linington/'Anne Blaisdell') include *Date With Death*, *Policeman's Lot* and *Perchance of Death*. The Mendoza books (by 'Dell Shannon' – over two dozen of them) include *The Ace of Spades*, *No Holiday for Crime*, *Cold Trail* and *Felony at Random*. The Varallo books (by 'Lesley Egan') include *A Case for Appeal* and *The Hunters and the Hunted*. The Falkenstein books (by 'Lesley Egan') include *Against the Evidence* and *The Wine of Life*.

LOCKED-ROOM MYSTERIES

Peter Anthony, *The Woman in the Wardrobe*
Lionel Black, *The Penny Murders*
▷ Anthony Boucher, *The Case of the Solid Key*
▷ Carter Dickson, *The Ten Teacups*
▷ Georgette Heyer, *Envious Casca*
▷ Maj Sjöwall and Per Wahlöö, *The Locked Room*
D.W. Smith, *Serious Crimes*
▷ Edgar Wallace, *Big Foot*

LONDON

▷Margery Allingham, *The Tiger in the Smoke*
▷Robert Barnard, *Bodies*
▷Gwendoline Butler, *Coffin in Fashion*
▷Arthur Conan Doyle, *A Study in Scarlet*
  Lettice Cooper, *Unusual Behaviour*
▷Dan Kavanagh, *Duffy*
▷Peter Lovesey, *Bertie and the Tin Man*
▷J.J. Marric, *Gideon's Day*
  Derek Raymond, *The Devil's Home on Leave*
  Jeremy Sturrock, *The Village of Rogues* (eighteenth century)

LOVESEY, Peter • (born 1936)
English writer

Lovesey's main detectives are two Victorian London police-men, Sergeant Cribb and Constable Thackeray. They combine thorough use of the then new-fangled 'scientific' methods of deduction (sometimes out-Sherlocking Holmes) with flashes of inspiration and a straight-faced irreverence towards their superiors and the pompous middle-class boors whose misdeeds they are uncovering. Each book is set in a different situation, and contains fascinating background of some characteristic activity of the Victorian English: walking races (*Wobble to Death*), the music-hall (*Abracadaver*), spiritualism (*A Case of Spirits*), prize-fighting (*The Detective Wore Silk Drawers*).

Lovesey has also written two books (*Bertie and the Tin Man*, *Bertie and the Seven Bodies*) in which the detective is no less a personage than Queen Victoria's son, the future King Edward VII.

 Read on

▶ Francis Selwyn, *Sergeant Verity and the Imperial Diamond*; Ray Harrison, *French Ordinary Murder*; Jean Stubbs, *Dear Laura*; Donald Thomas, *Belladonna*.

LUDLUM, Robert • (born 1927)
US writer

Early experience as an actor sharpened Ludlum's feeling for snappy dialogue, a major pleasure in his books. They explore the interplay between private and public intrigue, and blend imaginary characters and events with those of real life, to unnerving effect. He writes of a world just one step removed from ours: a world where political intrigue is an end in itself,

 Read on

● *The Gemini Contenders* (a huge, epic story spanning the last 50 years, centring on the search for secret documents supposedly proving that an impostor, not Christ, was

where lawlessness can be justified as 'for the greater good'. Coverups, bribery, 'necessary killings' – all are ways to prevent financial catastrophe or global war. Ludlum's central characters often begin by being drawn into machinations and manipulations which they have to puzzle out, and end by being isolated and hunted by both sides.

THE PARSIFAL MOSAIC (1982)

'Burnt out' CIA agent Michael Havelock, manipulated into believing his girlfriend a terrorist, arranges her murder – only to discover, when he leaves the agency, that she is still alive. He joins her in unmasking a conspiracy (led by a madman codenamed 'Parsifal', a senior politician) which will otherwise trigger the third world war.

Ludlum's thrillers include *The Scarlatti Inheritance*, *The Osterman Weekend*, *The Bourne Identity* (and its sequels *The Bourne Supremacy* and *The Bourne Ultimatum*), *The Matarese Circle*, *The Aquitaine Progression* and *Trevayne*. Some books appeared under the pseudonyms 'Jonathan Ryder' and 'Michael Shepherd', but have been republished under his own name.

LYALL, Gavin ● (born 1932)
English writer

The heroes of Lyall's adventure thrillers (until the 1980s a different person in each book; after 1980 Major Harry Maxin of British Army Intelligence) travel up to, and sometimes over, the brink of what is legal. Several stories (*The Wrong Side of the Sky*, *The Most Dangerous Game*, *Shooting Script*, *Judas Country*) involve flying, and their charter-pilot heroes accept dangerous cargoes or venture into 'no go' areas. *The Most Dangerous Game* (1964) culminates in the hero being hunted in Arctic Finland. In *Shooting Script* (1966) a film company pilot in the Caribbean finds real-life heroics overtaking fiction. When the pilot in *Judas Country* (1975) agrees to transport arms he quickly becomes involved in smuggling, Middle Eastern politics and association with people whose idea of moral behaviour is to double-cross or kill everyone in sight. In all Lyall's thrillers, the backgrounds are meticulously researched, the characters (especially politicians and bureaucrats) are brilliantly evoked, and the women (unlike those in some other adventure stories) are believable human beings.

crucified, and that the Christian religion is based on fraud).
▶ Allen Drury, *The Roads of Earth*; ▷Tom Clancy, *The Cardinal of the Kremlin*; Fred Taylor, *Walking Shadows* (set among German officers during the second world war); ▷Dan Sherman, *Dynasty of Spies*.

 Read on

● *The Conduct of Major Maxin.*
▶ ▷Craig Thomas, *Firefox*; ▷Peter Driscoll, *The Barboza Credentials*; ▷Desmond Bagley, *Juggernaut.*

LYALL

UNCLE TARGET (1988)

A British prototype tank is on loan to an (unspecified) Middle Eastern country when part of the country's army rebels. Major Maxin is flown in to blow up the tank before the rebels get it – and instead, he and a more or less untrained crew are forced to drive it across the desert to another Middle Eastern country, 'Saudia'.

Lyall's other thrillers include *Midnight Plus One, Venus With Pistol, Blame the Dead* and *The Secret Servant*.

M

MACABRE

▷Pierre Boileau and Thomas Narcejac, *Choice Cuts*
Ramsa Campbell, *Ancient Images*
▷William Haggard, *The Heirloom*
James Herbert, *Moon*
Stephen King, *Salem's Lot*
▷Ruth Rendell, *Live Flesh*

MacDONALD, John D(ann) (1916–86)
US writer

MacDonald is best known for his novels starring Travis McGee, a large, humorous ex-footballer who lives on a houseboat in Florida and goes out of 'retirement' to 'salvage' people in distress – to save them from crooks or avenge wrongs done to them. Although McGee's investigations are like those of a private eye, he sees himself as more like a knight errant of old, a Sir Galahad or Sir Lancelot, on the side of right against the evil in the world. MacDonald's plots are tortuous, the action is fast and tough, and McGee is as handy with one-liners as with his fists.

ONE FEARFUL YELLOW EYE (1966)
A famous surgeon, dying of a wasting disease, has squandered the $600,000 he was supposed to be leaving to his new young wife and his two bitter, grownup children. Why? McGee sets out to help the wife (an old friend), recover the money and patch up the family quarrel – a quest which grows ever more complicated and life-threatening, until the final, least expected and potentially most deadly twist of all.

 Read on

- *Pale Gray for Guilt.*
▶ **To the McGee books:**
  ▷Ross Macdonald, *The Underground Man*
  Cornelius Hirschberg, *Florentine Finish*; Colin Dunne, *Hooligan.*
▶ **To MacDonald's non-McGee novels:**
  ▷James M. Cain, *Double Indemnity*; John Gregory Dunne, *The Red White and Blue.*

All MacDonald's McGee books have a colour in the title: *The Quick Red Fox*, *A Deadly Shade of Gold*, *The Girl in the Plain Brown Wrapper*, *The Empty Copper Sea*, and so on. He is also the author of some 50 other crime novels, including *A Bullet for Cinderella*, *The Price of Murder*, *Soft Touch* and *The Last One Left*. They are good, but miss the 'classic' status of the McGee books.

MacDONALD, Philip • (1899–1981)
English writer

One of the great names of the 1930s and 1940s 'golden age', MacDonald is now neglected. The loss is ours, for his books – part thriller, part detection – are still reliably entertaining, and two (*Murder Gone Mad*, 1931; *X v Rex*/*Mystery of the Dead Police*/*The Mystery of Mister X*, 1934) are claimed by addicts to be among the finest in the genre. Most of his novels star the cool, stiff-upper-lip super-sleuth Anthony Gethryn, and are set in murky city backstreets or, ▷Buchan-like, in the wild British countryside. In MacDonald's best known book, *The List of Adrian Messenger* (1959), a man makes a list of ten names and is then killed in a plane crash. There is a macabre connection between the names, and Gethryn must find out what it is before every single person mentioned, and dozens of innocent bystanders, meet their deaths.

MacDonald's other books (some originally published under the pseudonym 'Martin Porlock') include *The Noose*, *The Choice*, *Persons Unknown*, *Rope to Spare* and *The Nursemaid Who Disappeared*/*Warrant for X*.

 Read on

- *Guest in the House*. In this satisfying, non-Gethryn story, a woman's ex-husband is blackmailing her by threatening, quite legally, to take their daughter. It is up to Colonel Ivor St George, the down-on-his-luck British house-guest, to find a way to stop him.
- ▶ ▷David Dodge, *The Long Escape*; Nicolas Bentley, *Third Party Crime*; ▷Anthony Berkeley, *Trial and Error*.

MACDONALD, Ross • (1915–83)
US writer

'Ross Macdonald' and 'John Ross Macdonald' are pseudonyms used by Kenneth Millar. His Lew Archer books are atmospheric private-eye thrillers, with a hypnotic, leisurely pace, a likeable and human Californian detective, tortuous plots and casts of marvellously eccentric secondary characters. Unlike Philip Marlowe or Sam Spade, to whom he is regularly compared, Lew Archer is an ordinary man, more likely to use psychology or simple patience to unmask the villains than to resort to violence or intrigue. One of

 Read on

- *The Galton Case*; *The Instant Enemy*.
- ▶ Thomas B. Dewey, *A Sad Song Singing*; ▷Joseph Hansen, *The Man Everybody Was Afraid Of*; ▷John Milne, *Daddy's Girl*; ▷Howard Engel, *A City Called July*.

Macdonald's greatest strengths is that he never resorts to melodramatic plotting or stagy dialogue.

THE UNDERGROUND MAN (1971)
The novel begins, typically for Macdonald, with Archer giving a small child peanuts to feed to jays on his front lawn. Almost at once he is called in to find the child's missing father, and begins to uncover a nest of lies, treachery and murder spreading back over 15 years and taking in half a dozen families. The case is complicated first by a (non-accidental) forest fire, and then when the child is kidnapped by two desperate, deluded teenagers on a stolen boat.

Macdonald's Archer novels include *The Moving Target/Harper*, *The Drowning Pool*, *The Zebra-Striped Hearse*, *The Goodbye Look*, *Find a Victim* and *Sleeping Beauty*. Millar also wrote non-Archer books: *The Ferguson Affair* and *The Wycherley Woman* as 'John Macdonald', and, under his own name, four books starring Chet Gordon.

MacINNES, Helen • (born 1907)
Scottish/US writer

Read on

▶ ▷Palma Harcourt, *Limited Options*; Anne Bridge, *The Episode at Toledo*; M.M. Kaye, *Death in Berlin*.

Many of MacInnes' two dozen adventure thrillers use the same brilliantly simple formula. An innocent person (musician; newspaperman; art-buyer in an auction room) is caught up in complicated and incomprehensible happenings – usually involving spies – in some well-researched foreign location. (MacInnes is especially good at describing such European cities as Geneva, Venice or Vienna.) The stories are told through the eyes of MacInnes' main characters, so that we share each discovery they make about plot, location and villains, moment by moment, in a way which makes the books easy but compulsive reads. Her novels include *Decision at Delphi*, *The Double Image*, *The Salzburg Connection*, *Snare of the Hunter*, *Prelude to Terror* and *The Venetian Affair* (1963), a cold-war thriller set in Rome and Venice, in which US journalist Bill Fenner, persuaded to act with the CIA against Communist subversives, meets Claire Connor – who is not what she first seems.

MacLEAN, Alistair • (born 1920)
Scottish/Swiss writer

Read on

• *Breakhart Pass*; *Goodbye California*.

Many of MacLean's all-action adventure stories are set in

wartime, and describe deeds of great daring or endurance. *The Guns of Navarone* (1957) and *Ice Station Zebra* (1963) are typical. *The Guns of Navarone* centres on the rescue of 1200 British soldiers from a small Greek island under the noses of German guns – a venture which requires the commandos to climb sheer cliffs, unseen, and blow up the guns. *Ice Station Zebra* is a cold-war story about a submarine sent to recover secret data recorded by a Russian spy satellite, which becomes trapped under the Arctic ice.

MacLean's two dozen best-sellers include *Fear Is the Key*, *When Eight Bells Toll*, *Where Eagles Dare*, *Breakhart Pass* and *Seawitch*. He has also written thrillers as 'Ian Stuart'; they include *Flood Tide*, *Sand Trap*, *Fatal Switch* and *A Weekend to Kill*.

▶ Nicholas Monsarrat, *The Cruel Sea*; ▷Wilbur Smith, *Hungry is the Sea*; ▷Hammond Innes, *Maddon's Rock/Gale Warning*.

MacLEOD, Charlotte • (born 1922)
Canadian/US writer

 Read on

MacLeod's breezy comedy mysteries centre on two groups of recurring characters. Her Professor Shandy books are set in Balaclava Agricultural College, Massachusetts, and draw on the teaching staff. MacLeod has fun, just in passing, with peoples' names, no-nonsense Scandinavian American ladies who look like Botticelli angels, and the politics of education. Professor Shandy and his wife are quiet, rational people, whose placid domestic life is thrown into high relief by the extraordinary personalities about them. The Sarah Kelling books are set among Boston's upper crust. Kelling and Max Bittersohn solve murder mysteries often connected with art and with the philanthropic, leisured world of the widespread Kelling clan. MacLeod uses the 'English' tendency of her Bostonians to recall and send up the conventions of English 'golden age' detective stories. She also writes children's books, romances (as 'Matilda Hughes') and comedy thrillers as 'Alisa Craig' (*A Pint of Murder*, *Murder Goes Mumming*).

MacLeod's books include *The Fat Lady's Ghost*, *Ask Me No Questions*, *We Dare Not Go A-Hunting*, *Rack and Rune* and *The Gladstone Bag*.

VANE PURSUIT (1989)
Shandy investigates the disappearance of weathervanes designed by Praxiteles Lumpkin. The story zestfully includes

● *The Palace Guard* (in which Kelling and Bittersohn, visiting a palatial museum owned by an enemy of the Kelling family, are astonished when a security guard falls past their window to his death – the start of a quest among dozens of ridiculous, exotic characters to unmask a forger, find a murderer and settle once and for all the question 'Are they the same person?').
▶ Alice Tilton, *Proof of the Pudding*; ▷Pamela Branch, *Murder's Little Sister*; ▷Delano Ames, *Murder, Maestro Please*.

fascist survivalists, a millionaire frozen to await as yet undreamed-of medical advances, whale-watching, arson, and a resourceful lady who lives below ground for several years. A plus for middle-aged fatties: anyone who is anyone in this book is over 40, and several are also overweight – and happy.

MAFIA

▷Andrew Coburn, *Sweetheart*
▷Richard Condon, *Prizzi's Honour*
▷Paul Erdman, *The Palace*
▷Michael Gilbert, *The Long Journey Home*
▷Jack Higgins, *Luciano's Luck*
▷Robert Ludlum, *The Gemini Contenders*
  J. Lynn, *Factory*
  G.F. Newman, *Man With the Guns*
  Lawrence Sanders, *Caper*
▷Mickey Spillane, *The Last Cop Out*
▷Donald E. Westlake, *The Busy Body*

MALING, Arthur • (born 1923)
US writer

In each of Maling's thoughtful, well-paced crime thrillers an ordinary person becomes innocently involved with crime, and has to battle ever-increasing danger and violence before he or she can work out what is happening and why, and bring the situation to a proper conclusion. Many of the novels concern financial corruption, and the crime is often on a national or international scale. Half a dozen books star Brock Potter, head of a New York brokerage firm – but the plot's strands and preoccupations are the same as in Maling's non-series thrillers. Maling beautifully handles the way family and love relationships are threatened or destroyed by the outside forces ranged against his heroes.

Maling's non-series thrillers include *Decoy*, *Go-Between*, *Loophole*, *Dingdong* and *The Rheingold Route*. His Potter books include *Ripoff*, *Schroeder's Game*, *The Koberg Link* and *A Taste of Treason*.

 Read on

▶ **To Maling's Potter books:** ▷David Dodge, *Shear the Black Sheep*; ▷Emma Lathen, *Pick Up Sticks*; ▷Paul Erdman, *The Billion Dollar Killing/The Billion Dollar Sure Thing*.
▶ **To his non-series thrillers:** ▷George Sims, *The Last Best Friend*; ▷Margaret Millar, *Ask For Me Tomorrow*; ▷Michael Gilbert, *The Long Journey Home*.

MANN, Jessica
English writer

Mann says that she likes to write, and read, books which concentrate on 'people, places and puzzles, in that order'. Her pacy, intelligent novels (a smooth blend of mystery and thriller) take off like rockets, and each explanation leads to even greater mystification. We are intrigued by her characters – especially her heroine, the resourceful but all-too-human detective/secret agent Tamara Hoyland – and read on not only to unravel the plot but to find out more about them. Her books include *Mrs Knox's Profession*, *The Sticking Place*, *The Eighth Deadly Sin*, *The Sting of Death* and *Death Beyond the Nile* (1988), in which Hoyland is hired to keep an eye on one member of a tourist group in Egypt – a woman who has discovered a way to induce mass epilepsy, and who is at risk from people who want to develop it as a battle-weapon instead of (as she does) for medical purposes.

MARLOWE, Hugh
see PATTERSON, Henry

MARRIC, J.J.
see CREASEY, John

MARSH, Ngaio • (1899–1982)
New Zealand writer

Few authors handle the 'classic' detective story as well as Marsh. The murder methods in her books are ingenious, unexpected and gruesome. The locations are fascinating: during a village-hall concert, in the shearing-shed of a sheep farm, among Satanists in a villa in France, at a diplomatic reception and, above all – reflecting her own passionate interest in drama – backstage, in the wings and onstage at theatres. Her theatre books (*Enter A Murderer*, *Opening Night*, *Vintage Murder*, *Death at the Dolphin/Killer Dolphin*) are among her wittiest. She was fond of exotic characters, especially artists, preening actors and the upper class. Her detection is scrupulously fair, with every clue appearing to the reader at the same time as to Alleyn, Marsh's urbane and hawk-eyed sleuth. Above all, her books move at a furious pace, fuelled by her glee at the fantasies and follies of humankind.

 Read on

- *Captive Audience*; *Funeral Sites*.
- ▷ Joan Aiken, *Last Movement*; S.F.X. Dean, *By Frequent Anguish*; Joan Smith, *Masculine Ending*.

 Read on

- *Final Curtain*.
- **To *A Surfeit of Lampreys*:** ▷ Margery Allingham, *The Beckoning Lady*; ▷ P.D. James, *A Taste for Death*; ▷ Jean Potts, *Go, Lovely Rose*.
- **To Marsh's books with theatrical settings:** ▷ Michael Innes, *Hamlet, Revenge*; ▷ Simon Brett, *Cast, in Order of Disappearance*; Caroline Graham, *Death of a Hollow Man*.
- **To Marsh's books in general:** ▷ H.R.F. Keating, *Zen There Was Murder*; Elizabeth

A SURFEIT OF LAMPREYS/DEATH OF A PEER (1947)
The Lampreys are a large upper-class English family, devoted
to one another and fond of private jokes, charades and a self-
consciously eccentric approach to life. They are also broke.
They invite grim, unsmiling Uncle Gabriel to their flat to
borrow money from him – and he is murdered in the lift.
Alleyn's task is not just to work out how the murder was
done (and who dunnit), but also to pick his way through the
maze of false clues, red herrings and downright lies which
the Lampreys amuse themselves by telling him.

Apart from those mentioned, Marsh's three dozen books
include *Death in Ecstasy, Artists in Crime, Overture to Death,
Death and the Dancing Footman, Colour Scheme, Spinsters in
Jeopardy/The Bride of Death, Hand in Glove* and *Clutch of
Constables.*

MARSHALL, Raymond
see CHASE, James Hadley

McBAIN, Ed
see HUNTER, Evan

McCLOY, Helen ● (born 1904)
US writer

McCloy wrote a dozen 'classic' crime thrillers starring the
psychiatrist Dr Basil Willing, who uses his scientific skills to
discover motives and uncover clues. Her other books are
psychological thrillers, studies of people trapped not just by
circumstances but by their own feelings of unfocused,
terrifying guilt.

THE SLAYER AND THE SLAIN (1957)
The story begins when the narrator slips on an icy pavement
and is treated for concussion. Later, looking into a mirror, he
sees that he seems to have aged – and as the book proceeds,
he is drawn ever deeper into bewilderment, a man he hates
is mysteriously murdered and he himself begins receiving
anonymous letters . . .

McCloy's Willing books include *Dance of Death/Design for
Dying, The Deadly Truth, The Goblin Market* and *Mr Splitfoot.*

Lemarchand, *Step in the
Dark*; ▷Peter Dickinson,
The Poison Oracle.

 Read on

● *The Long Body* (Willing);
  Through a Glass, Darkly
  (psychological).
▶ To the Willing books:
  ▷Ellery Queen, *The Greek
  Coffin Mystery.*
▶ To the psychological
  thrillers: B.M. Gill,
  Victims; ▷Celia Fremlin,
  *Appointment With
  Yesterday*; ▷Margaret
  Yorke, *Safely to the
  Grave*; ▷Ira Levin, *A Kiss
  Before Dying.*

Her psychological thrillers include *A Change of Heart*, *The Sleepwalker*, *Minotaur Country* and *The Smoking Mirror*. *The Singing Diamond/Surprise Surprise* is a collection of short stories.

McCLURE, James ● (born 1939)
South African/English writer

McClure's quietly written stories star Lieutenant Kramer and Sergeant Zondi of the Trekkersburg Murder and Robbery Squad in small-town South Africa. They are buddies, their deep trust and friendship masked by banter. Their investigations take them into some of the murkiest corners of South African life (for example terrorism and neo-Nazi politics). So far, so efficient – but the books' whole point is that Kramer is white and Zondi is black. The mutual respect and dignity of their friendship are in marked contrast to the unthinking racism all round them, and give McClure's books an edge which is all the sharper because of his understated, unhysterical style. His novels include *The Steam Pig*, *Four and Twenty Virgins*, *The Gooseberry Fool*, *Snake*, *Rogue Eagle* and *The Sunday Hangman* (1977), which begins when a condemned man is taken out and hanged – not by the state executioner but by a highly efficient amateur.

Read on

- *The Blood of an Englishman; The Artful Egg.*
- ▶ Books with a South African crime setting: June Drummond, *I Saw Him Die*; ▷Wessel Ebersohn, *A Lonely Place to Die*; Tom Sharpe, *Indecent Exposure* (satirical farce).

McCRUM, Robert
English writer

McCrum's books are part thriller, part 'literary' novel. Their backgrounds are politics, sometimes espionage, and the pace is fast, but they explore themes of identity and motive more deeply than most thrillers do. *In the Secret State* (1980), for example, set in a Britain stalked by terrorists, begins with the discovery of a corpse. Frank Strange, on his last day in British Intelligence, wonders if the death may explain political undercurrents in the department which have led to his forced resignation. During the ensuing investigation he, and everyone he meets, confronts the questions of the legal accountability of a secret service, and of the conflict of loyalties to friends, colleagues and country.

Read on

- *The Fabulous Englishman* (which intercuts the story of the growing-up of Christopher Iles in England with events in Czechoslovakia from 1968. Much is revealed by letters from a Czech bookseller unknown to Iles – and the rollercoaster ride begins when the two men agree to meet).
- ▶ ▷John Le Carré, *The Russia House*; ▷Dan Sherman, *The Prince of Berlin*; ▷Andrew Taylor, *Black List*; ▷John Crosby, *Snake*.

McCUTCHAN, Philip • (born 1920)

English writer

Under his own name, McCutchan is known for three series of action thrillers, each a good follow-up to the others. The Commander Shaw books star an ex-navy officer now working for a hush-hush commando unit. The Simon Shard books feature a senior London policeman seconded to the Foreign Office (where he investigates cases of terrorism, kidnapping and espionage). The Lieutenant Halfhyde books (for example *Halfhyde to the Narrows*, *Halfhyde for the Queen*) are about a naval officer in the 1890s, the early days of steam. Under the pseudonym 'Robert Conington Galway' McCutchan has written a series about James Packard, an adventurer modelled on James Bond. As 'Duncan MacNeil' he has written a fifth series, starring an Indian army officer of about 100 years ago. These include *Drums Along the Khyber* and *The Mullah from Kashmir*.

McCutchan's Shaw books include *Warmaster*, *This Drakotny* and *Sunstrike*. His Shard books include *A Very Big Bang*, *The Eros Affair* and *Blackmail North*. His Packard books include *Assignment New York*, *Assignment Malta* and *Assignment Sydney*.

MCDONALD

 Read on

▶ To McCutchan's Shaw books: Nicholas Luard, *Travelling Horseman*.
▶ To his Shard books: ▷John Creasey, *The Enemy Within*.
▶ To his Packard books: ▷Ian Fleming, *Doctor No*.

MCDONALD, Gregory • (born 1937)

US writer

Mcdonald's 'Fletch' books are mystery farces, starring the amiable newspaper reporter Irwin Maurice Fletcher. Fletch likes to bob on the surface of life like a cork in a running stream. Each book begins with a complete surprise – a millionaire offers Fletch a fortune to murder him, a murdered woman is discovered in his locked apartment, a letter from his 'dead' father invites him and his new wife to Kenya when they planned to spend their honeymoon skiing in Colorado. Each time, Fletch follows the surprise wherever it leads, into ever more sinister, and slapstick, adventures. The 'Flynn' series stars a Boston police inspector who is also a special agent, and who is called in to solve cases with international political implications or involving VIPs (in *The Buck Passes Flynn*, the President himself). Flynn's cases, like Fletch's, spiral from one unlikely event to another. But the Flynn books are thrillers rather than farces, with the jokes coming from the characters rather than from ludicrous events.

 Read on

▶ **To Mcdonald's Fletch books:** ▷Lawrence Block, *Burglars Can't Be Choosers*; ▷Donald E. Westlake and ▷Brian Garfield, *Gangway!*.
▶ **To the Flynn books:** ▷Robert B. Parker, *The Godwulf Manuscript*; ▷John D. MacDonald, *The Quick Red Fox*.

MEDIA

The Fletch books (which can be read in any order, though they form a chronological sequence) are *Fletch Won, Fletch Too, Fletch and the Widow Bradley, Fletch, Carioca Fletch, Confess Fletch, Fletch's Fortune, Fletch's Moxie* and *Fletch and the Man Who*. The Flynn books are *Flynn, The Buck Passes Flynn* and *Flynn's In*. Mcdonald has also written non-series novels (*Running Scared, Safekeeping*) and a volume of autobiography, *The Education of Gregory Mcdonald*.

MEDIA
(newspapers; magazines; advertising agencies)

▷Joan Aiken, *Trouble With Product X*
▷Pamela Branch, *Murder's Little Sister*
  Lillian Jackson Braun, *The Cat Who Could Read Backwards*
  Eric Bruton, *Death in Ten Point Bold*
  Dorothy Salisbury Davis, *Lullaby of Murder*
  Lesley Grant-Adamson, *Wild Justice*
▷Robert Harling, *The Enormous Shadow*
  Tim Heald, *Deadline*
  Charles Larson, *Muir's Blood*
  Minette Marin, *The Eye of the Beholder*
  E. and M.A. Radford, *Death of a Frightened Editor*
▷Dorothy L. Sayers, *Murder Must Advertise*
▷Donald E. Westlake, *Trust Me on This*

MELVILLE, James • (born 1931)
English writer

'James Melville' is the pseudonym of Roy Peter Martin. His Commissioner Otani is the Maigret of Hyogo Prefecture in Japan – a placid, middle-aged man, happily married, solving crimes not by melodramatic re-stagings but by gentle, patient probing. For the non-Japanese, the books have plenty of exotic detail – a great deal of sushi is consumed by people sitting on tatami mats – but the main interest is in the characters of Otani himself, his wife Hanae and his inspectors, man-about-town Kimura and bovine-seeming 'Ninja' Noguchi. The clash between cultures caused by foreigners visiting Japan is a theme in many books, for

 Read on

▶ Masako Togawa, *Lady Killer*; ▷Georges Simenon, *Madame Maigret's Friend*; ▷H.R.F. Keating, *Filmi, Filmi, Inspector Ghote*.

example *The Wages of Zen* (1979), about murder in a monastery, and *Kimono for a Corpse* (1987), about extortion and murder in a high-fashion business. Melville's other Otani books include *A Sort of Samurai, Sayonara Sweet Amaryllis, Death of a Daimyo, The Death Ceremony* and *A Haiku for Hanae*.

MELVILLE, Jennie
see BUTLER, Gwendoline

MIDDLE EAST

▷Lionel Davidson, *A Long Way to Shiloh/The Menorah Man*
   Michael Delahaye, *Third Day*
▷James Follett, *Mirage*
▷Jonathan Kellerman, *Butcher's Theatre*
▷John le Carré, *The Little Drummer Girl*
▷Blaine Littell, *The Dolorosa Deal*
▷Gavin Lyall, *Judas Country*
▷Clive Sinclair, *Cosmetic Effects*
▷Wilbur Smith, *Eagle in the Sky*
   Leon Uris, *Exodus*

MILLAR, Margaret ● (born 1915)
Canadian writer

Millar is best known for psychological crime stories, usually set in small communities and among close-knit families or ethnic groups. She is fascinated by the way crime exposes the raw nerves and guts of people's characters, and spends less time solving the mystery (though that is done in passing) than in detailing how each member of a group only begins to reveal his or her true nature once the deed is done. To this onion-skinning psychological investigation she adds the pleasure of satire – although her books are serious, she is happy to send up her characters if their obsessions or behaviour ask for it.

SPIDER WEBS (1986)
In a California court, Cully King is on trial for murder. The

Read on

● *The Banshee.*
▶ Dorothy Salisbury Davis, *Lullaby of Murder;* Helen Nielsen, *Sing Me a Murder;* ▷Ross Macdonald (Margaret Millar's husband), *The Underground Man.*

judge is eccentric, the district attorney is a domestic tyrant, the defence attorney has a crazy wife – and as for the witnesses . . . As the trial proceeds, Millar shows us each person's obsessions in turn – and brings both trial and story to a surprise conclusion, a twist within a twist, which not even Perry Mason could have stage-managed.

Millar's books include *Wall of Eyes*, *Beast in View*, *The Fiend*, *Beyond This Point Are Monsters*, *The Murder of Miranda* and *Mermaid*.

MILNE, John • (born 1952)
English writer

After three conventional novels (*London Fields*, *Out of the Blue* and *Tyro*) Milne began a series starring Jimmy Jenner, a one-legged, streetwise London private eye – and one of the best crime-thriller heroes since Philip Marlowe hung up his hat. Whenever Jenner picks up his phone, he enters a labyrinth of betrayals, beatings-up, quadruple bluff and equivocal encounters with beautiful girls, world-weary cops and corpses not quite so dead as they ought to be. The books fizz along, propelled not by ▷Chandleresque wisecracks but by a peculiarly English, peculiarly 1990s combination of irony and irritability. Milne's Jenner novels, so far, are *Dead Birds*, *Shadow Play* and *Daddy's Girl*.

 Read on

▶ Sara Paretsky, *Indemnity Only*; ▷Loren D. Estleman, *Angel Eyes*; Robert Crais, *The Monkey's Raincoat*; Peter Corris, *The Marvellous Boy*.

MINDSICK

John Franklin Bardin, *The Deadly Percheron*
James Barnett, *Diminished Responsibility*
John Bingham, *Five Roundabouts to Heaven*
▷Robert Bloch, *Psycho*
▷W.J. Burley, *The Schoolmaster*
▷Vera Caspary, *Bedelia*
▷Anna Clarke, *One of Us Must Die*
▷Andrew Coburn, *Goldilocks*
▷C.S. Forester, *Payment Deferred*
▷Celia Fremlin, *The Spider-Orchid*
▷Francis Iles, *Malice Aforethought*
▷Georges Simenon, *The Hatter's Ghosts*
Roger L. Simon, *Heir*
Deborah Valentine, *A Collector of Photographs*

MITCHELL, Gladys • (1901–83)
English writer

Mitchell's detective, Mrs (later Dame) Beatrice Adela Lestrange Bradley, 'a pterodactyl with a Cheshire Cat smile', stars in over 50 novels, beginning with *Speedy Death* (1929). She is as near a witch as anyone can be without being arrested, and solves bizarre crimes many of which involve ghosts, skeletons and dark doings in ancient British burial grounds by dead of night. In many books, she is assisted by Laura Menzies, a galumphing, slang-spouting, jolly-hockey-sticks Scottish lass who is forever striding over moors or stripping off her clothes to swim across fast-flowing rivers. Mitchell plants every clue fairly, so that you can solve the mystery ahead of Dame Beatrice, if you dare.

THE TWENTY-THIRD MAN (1957)
A popular tourist sight, of 23 embalmed kings sitting round a table, becomes even more macabre when a 24th body joins them just as one of the hotel guests vanishes. Dame Beatrice, on holiday in Capri, investigates means, motive and opportunity, opening one of the nastiest cans of worms of her whole career.

Good Dame Beatrice novels are *Come Away Death*, *Laurels are Poison*, *Spotted Hemlock*, *Twelve Horses and the Hangman's Noose* and *Say it with Flowers*. Mitchell also wrote crime books under the pseudonym 'Malcolm Torrie'; they star Timothy Herring, president of the quintessentially English Society for the Preservation of Ancient Buildings. Typical examples are *Late and Cold*, *Churchyard Salad* and *Bismarck Herrings*.

MOFFAT, Gwen • (born 1924)
English writer

Moffat worked as a climbing guide, and the climaxes of her Miss Pink detective stories usually take place on mountains. Miss Pink is an elderly justice of the peace, interested in wild places. She is an eager camper, rider, walker, bird-watcher and (when arthritis allows) climber. Wherever she goes – the Cuillins of Skye, the Arizona desert, the English Lake District – evil lurks, and her enjoyment of the environment has to take second place as she investigates some spectacular piece of human nastiness. Moffat's Miss Pink books include

 Read on

- *Three Quick and Five Dead.*
- ▷ Michael Innes, *Lament for a Maker*; ▷ John Dickson Carr, *Below Suspicion*; ▷ Colin Watson, *The Naked Nuns*.

 Read on

- ▷ Arthur Upfield, *The Mountains Have a Secret* (set in Australia); ▷ Joe Gores, *Come Morning* (putting mountain-climbing skills to a most ingenious use); ▷ Gladys Mitchell, *Ten Horsemen and the Hangman's Noose* (featuring that similarly

Lady With a Cool Eye, Miss Pink at the Edge of the World, Over the Sea to Death, Persons Unknown, Die Like a Dog and *Last Chance Country.* She has also published two non-Pink novels, with the same kind of story-line – *Deviant Death* and *The Corpse Road.*

formidable elderly detective, Dame Beatrice Bradley).

MONASTERIES

▷Peter Dickinson, *The Seals/The Sinful Stones*
▷Umberto Eco, *The Name of the Rose*
▷Colin Forbes, *The Heights of Zervos*
▷James Melville, *The Wages of Zen*
  J. O'Hagan, *Death and a Madonna*
▷Ellis Peters, *A Morbid Taste for Bones*
  J. Reeves, *Murder Before Matins*
▷Donald E. Westlake, *Brothers Keepers*

MORLAND, Dick
see HILL, Reginald

MORTON, Anthony
see CREASEY, John

MOSS, Robert • (born 1946)
US writer

Moss's thrillers are packed with research: even the smell of a particular brand of cigarette in downtown Caracas or the kind of paperclips used by third-grade Kremlin clerks is described exactly. Rightly or wrongly, this gives the books a feeling of documentary truth – a feeling increased by Moss's thoughtful descriptions of his characters' private lives and feelings. Add tension and fast action to all this, and the result is rich and rare. His best known book, *Moscow Rules* (1985), describes the planning and execution of an abortive Kremlin coup in the years just before Gorbachev.

 Read on

- *Carnival of Spies* (set in the 1930s, and based on fact: about a young German, working for British Intelligence against the Nazis, who is sent to Brazil to organize a communist revolution, the setting up of the first-ever New World Stalinist state).
▶ Julian Semyonov, *Tass is Authorized to Announce*; Vladimir Volkoff, *The Set Up*; Robert Littell, *Mother Russia.*

MOUNTAINS

  Victor Canning, *Panther's Moon*
  Glyn Carr, *Murder of an Owl*
▷Jon Cleary, *The Pulse of Danger*
▷Joe Gores, *Come Morning*
  Duff Hart-Davis, *The Heights of Rimring*
▷Bob Langley, *Traverse of the Gods*
  Hugh McLeave, *Under the Icefall*
▷Gwen Moffat, *Miss Pink at the Edge of the World*
▷Trevanian, *The Eiger Sanction*

MOYES, Patricia • (born 1923)
Irish writer

Moyes' light-hearted crime stories star the Scotland Yard detective Henry Tibbett, and there is a vast supporting cast of his relatives, friends and colleagues. Each book is self-contained, but each gives more details of the Tibbett ménage, as if mysteries were being tacked on to gossipy family letters. Each book also sends Tibbett and his wife to a different location: a Swiss ski-lodge, the backstreets of Amsterdam, Hollywood (where Moyes once worked as Peter Ustinov's assistant), the Caribbean. The crimes and the perpetrators' motives are satisfyingly gruesome, but the stories themselves flow effortlessly along – detective novels as escapism have seldom been better done.

Moyes' books include *Dead Men Don't Ski*, *The Sunken Sailor/Down Among the Dead Men*, *Murder à la Mode*, *Falling Star*, *Death and the Dutch Uncle*, *Black Widower* and *To Kill a Coconut*.

Read on

▶ Jocelyn Davey, *Murder in Paradise;*
  ▷Magdalen Nabb, *Death in Autumn;*
  Marian Babson, *Murder, Murder, Little Star.*

MUSIC

▷Delano Ames, *Murder, Maestro Please*
▷J.R.L. Anderson, *Festival*
▷Robert Barnard, *Death and the Chaste Apprentice*
  Liza Cody, *Under Contract*
  Robert Goldsborough, *Murder in E Minor*
▷Cyril Hare, *When the Wind Blows/The Wind Blows Death*

MUSIC

S.T. Haymon, *Death of a God*
▷H.R.F. Keating, *Death of a Fat God*
Kenneth O'Hara, *The Searchers of the Dead*
▷Ellis Peters, *Black is the Colour of My True Love's Heart*

N

NABB, Magdalen • (born 1947)
English writer

Nabb's novels are set in Florence, and give as much pleasure for their beautifully described setting as for the ingenious mysteries Police Marshal Guernaccia is set to solve. Her books include *Death in Springtime, Death of a Dutchman, Death of an Englishman* and the particularly atmospheric *Death in Autumn* (1985).

  Read on

- *The Marshal's Own Case.*
▶ Timothy Holme, *The Neopolitan Streak;* ▷Georges Simenon, *Maigret's Pipe;* ▷H.R.F. Keating, *Inspector Ghote Trusts the Heart.*

NAZIS AND NAZI GOLD

▷Evelyn Anthony, *The Poellenberg Inheritance*
▷Desmond Bagley, *The Golden Keel*
▷Frederick Forsyth, *The Odessa File*
▷Jack Higgins, *The Eagle Has Landed*
▷Geoffrey Jenkins, *Southtrap*
▷Duncan Kyle, *Black Camelot*
▷Bob Langley, *Autumn Tiger*
▷Robert Ludlum, *The Rhinemann Exchange*
▷Alistair MacLean, *River of Death*
  Frederick Nolan, *The Oshawa Project*
▷Elleston Trevor, *The Damocles Sword*
  Leon Uris, *QB VII*

NEW YORK

George Bagby, *Dirty Pool*
Richard Barth, *The Rag Bag Clan*

NEW YORK

▷Lawrence Block, *Burglars Can't Be Choosers*
▷Chester Himes, *Blind Man With a Pistol/Hot Day, Hot Night*
▷Ed McBain, *Give the Boys a Great Big Hand*
  Dorothy Uhnak, *The Bait*
▷Hillary Waugh, *Finish Me Off*
▷Donald E. Westlake, *A New York Dance/Dancing Aztecs*

OXBRIDGE

    Hosanna Brown, *I Spy, You Die*
▷Gwendoline Butler, *A Coffin for Pandora/Olivia*
▷Edmund Crispin, *The Case of the Gilded Fly/Obsequies at Oxford*
    Glyn Daniel, *The Cambridge Murders*
▷Antonia Fraser, *Oxford Blood*
▷Michael Innes, *Death at the President's Lodging*
▷P.D. James, *An Unsuitable Job for a Woman*
    J.C. Masterman, *An Oxford Tragedy*
    Robert Robinson, *Landscape with Dead Dons*
▷Dorothy L. Sayers, *Gaudy Night*

P

![gun illustration]

PARETSKY, Sara • (born 1947)
US writer

Paretsky's Chicago private eye, V.I. Warshawski, moves in a murky world of drug-trafficking, union corruption, medical fraud and religious politics. Warshawski is a crack shot, a karate expert, and has an armoury of bruisingly unanswerable one-liners. She is also devastatingly beautiful, and combines contempt for masculine bravado with a tendency to go weak at the knees whenever a gorgeous hunk swims into view.

The Warshawski books are *Indemnity Only*, *Deadlock*, *Killing Orders*, *Bitter Medicine*, *Toxic Shock* and *Burn Marks*.

 Read on

▶ Sue Grafton, *'A' is for Alibi*; ▷Loren D. Estleman, *Every Brilliant Eye*; ▷Rex Stout, *Crime on her Hands/The Hand in the Glove*; ▷John Milne, *Shadow Play*.

PARKER, Robert B(rown) • (born 1932)
US writer

Many writers of private-eye thrillers are claimed to be ▷Chandler's heir; Parker is the likeliest – and indeed has completed Chandler's last, unfinished Marlowe novel, *Poodle Springs*. His detective, Spenser, is as tough as Marlowe, as unafraid, and as much a master of the wisecrack. Boston stands in for Los Angeles, but the extortionists, curvaceous dames and filthy rich, stewing in the corruption of their wealth, are just the same. The Spenser books include *The Godwulf Manuscript*, *Mortal Stakes*, *Love and Glory*, *Playmates*, *Taming a Seahorse*, *Pale Kings and Princes* and *Crimson Joy*.

LOOKING FOR RACHEL WALLACE (1980)
Spenser is hired to look after the feminist writer Rachel Wallace on a speaking tour. She despises his macho attitude,

 Read on

• *The Judas Goat* (in which Spenser, hired to find the gang who murdered a rich man's wife and daughters, tracks them to London, Copenhagen, Amsterdam and Montreal – offering himself as bait).
▶ ▷Raymond Chandler, *Farewell My Lovely*; ▷John D. MacDonald, *A Tan and Sandy Silence*; ▷Sara Paretsky, *Indemnity Only*; Jonathan Valin, *Life's Work*; Peter Corris, *White Meat*.

and fires him. Then she is kidnapped – and Spenser sets out to find her, despite all attempts (by the police, his enemies and his girlfriend) to make him drop the case.

PARTNERS IN CRIME
(detective teams, usually related)

▷Delano Ames, *Corpse Diplomatique*
▷Agatha Christie, *N or M?*
  Hildegarde Dolson, *Beauty Sleep*
▷Francis Durbridge, *Paul Temple Intervenes*
▷Dashiell Hammett, *The Thin Man*
  Joseph Harrington, *The Last Known Address*
  Hilda Lawrence, *Death of a Doll*
▷Charlotte MacLeod, *The Palace Guard*
▷Patricia Moyes, *Dead Men Don't Ski*
▷Elizabeth Peters, *Lion in the Valley*
  Richard Powell, *All Over Bar the Shooting*
  Craig Rice, *The Corpse Steps Out*
  Kelley Roos, *Made Up to Kill*

PATRICK, Q.
see QUENTIN, Patrick

PATTERSON, Henry • (born 1929)
English writer

Patterson has published adventure thrillers under several names: Harry Patterson, Martin Fallon, James Graham, Hugh Marlowe and ▷Jack Higgins. All have been successful, but none more so than the 'Jack Higgins' books -- which has led to him republishing many of his other books as by Higgins. His stories are action-packed, violent and full of character. They make excellent follow-ups to one another. His 'Harry Patterson' books include *Pay the Devil*, *The Graveyard Shift* and *To Catch a King*. His 'Martin Fallon' books include *Year of the Tiger* and *A Prayer for the Dying*. His 'James Graham' books include *A Game for Heroes*, *The Khufra Run* and *Bloody Passage*. His 'Hugh Marlowe' books include *Seven Pillars to Hell* and *A Candle for the Dead/The Violent Enemy*. For his

'Jack Higgins' books, and for good follow-ups, see separate entry under Higgins.

PENSIONERS

  Josephine Bell, *Death in Retirement*
▷Simon Brett, *A Nice Class of Corpse*
▷Agatha Christie, *Postern of Fate*
  V.C. Clinton-Baddeley, *Death's Bright Dart*
▷Bob Cook, *Paper Chase*
  David Cook, *Missing Persons*
▷Henry Farrell, *What Ever Happened to Baby Jane?*
▷Dorothy Gilman, *The Unexpected Mrs Pollifax/Mrs Pollifax Spy*
  Arthur Goldstein, *A Person Shouldn't Die Like That*
▷Reginald Hill, *Exit Lines*
  John Lutz, *Kiss*
▷Charlotte MacLeod, *Recycled Citizen*

PENTECOST, Hugh • (born 1903)
US writer

'Hugh Pentecost' is the pseudonym of ▷Judson Philips. He is the author of over 100 crime novels, ranging from police procedurals to gangland thrillers. He is best known for two series. The Chambrun books star Pierre Chambrun, the manager of an expensive New York hotel who uses his wartime experience in the French Resistance to help him solve crimes committed in the hotel, often with international ramifications: espionage, drug-smuggling, terrorism. The Quist books star Julian Quist, public relations representative for a large financial house, who falls into crime – usually industrial espionage, kidnapping or fraud – both in his day-to-day work and whenever he tries to take a holiday.

The Chambrun novels include *Random Killer, Death After Breakfast, Birthday Deathday* and *The Cannibal Who Overate.* The Quist novels include *Deadly Trap, Die After Dark, Honeymoon With Death* and *The Homicidal Horse.*

 Read on

▶ ▷Dick Francis, *The Edge;* ▷Gregory Mcdonald, *Flynn;* ▷Ed McBain, *Snow White and Rose Red.*

PETERS, Elizabeth • (born 1927)
US writer

'Elizabeth Peters' is the crime-writing pseudonym of Barbara Mertz, who also publishes historical and supernatural stories as 'Barbara Michaels'. Her crime books are romantic mysteries, often using her interest in history and archaeology and strong on humour and parody. A good example is *Street of the Five Moons*, starring Vicky Bliss, whose work (she is an expert in medieval art) takes her to Rome – where she promptly becomes mixed up with forgers and falls in love. Peters' liveliest comedies (beginning with *The Curse of the Pharaohs*, 1981) feature the Victorian archaeologist and feminist Amelia Peabody and her husband Radcliffe Emerson. Peters has great fun combining Victorian English manners with modern ideas and turns of speech. In each book, Peabody and Emerson leave their home comforts to dig in Egypt, usually accompanied by their hyper-intelligent brat of a son Ramses. As soon as they arrive, a wonderfully bizarre supporting cast appears, cross-purposes abound and all hell breaks loose.

 Read on

- *Lion in the Valley* (Peabody); *Crocodile on the Sandbank* (non-Peabody).
- ▷ Dorothy Dunnett, *Dolly and the Starry Bird/Murder in Focus*; ▷ Charlotte MacLeod, *Vane Pursuit*; ▷ Delano Ames, *Murder, Maestro Please*.

PETERS, Ellis • (born 1913)
English writer

Romantic and historical novelist Edith Pargeter uses 'Ellis Peters' as a pseudonym for her crime novels. They are in two series, one starring the thirteenth-century monk Brother Cadfael, the other centring on the modern Felse family. Cadfael works in the herb garden of Shrewsbury Abbey, and each novel, as well as a murder and a romance, includes fascinating detail of some characteristic medieval activity – saint's-day celebration, fair, tournament and so on. The Felse books' main character is Dominic, the charming, music-loving son of police detective George Felse. As a teenager Dominic helps in his father's cases; when he is a young man, he and his girlfriend Tossa fall into mysteries (usually in romantic places like Capri, New Delhi and San Francisco) and George Felse helps to rescue them.

Both series are crammed with unusual characters and events. The Cadfael books include *A Morbid Taste for Bones*, *One Corpse too Many*, *Saint Peter's Fair* and *The Pilgrim of Hate* (1984), in which a murderer seeks sanctuary in the abbey just as the monks are engrossed in ceremonies connected with

 Read on

- *The Leper of St Giles* (Cadfael); *Death to the Landlords* (Felse).
- ▶ To *The Pilgrim of Hate*: Tom de Haan, *The Child of Good Fortune* (medieval); ▷ G.K. Chesterton, *The Innocence of Father Brown* (short stories: mysteries solved by a gentle priest).
- ▶ To *Mourning Raga*: M.M. Kaye, *Death in Kashmir*; ▷ Mary Stewart, *The Gabriel Hounds*.

the interment of sacred relics (St Winifred's bones). The Felse books include *Fallen into the Pit*, *Death and the Joyful Woman*, *A Nice Derangement of Epitaphs*, *Black is the Colour of my True Love's Heart* and *Mourning Raga* (1969) in which Dominic and Tossa, in New Delhi to return a young girl to her family, become involved with the Indian film industry – and with murder.

PHILIPS, Judson • (born 1903)
US writer

Philips also wrote under the pseudonym ▷Hugh Pentecost. Under his own name, he is best known for a series of novels and short stories starring the New York reporter Peter Styles. Styles is an innocent at large, stumbling his way through adventures, almost always being outsmarted and misreading the situation, but usually provoking the kidnappers, drug-pedlars, blackmailers and murderers he is dealing with into making one fatal mistake which brings the story to a dramatic and satisfying conclusion. The Styles books include *The Laughter Trap*, *The Wings of Madness*, *Hot Summer Killing*, *The Larkspur Conspiracy* and *Five Roads to Death* (1977), which begins when beautiful Lynn Mason asks Styles to investigate the (possibly faked) kidnapping of her boyfriend, a successful and charismatic young businessman.

Read on
▶ ▷Jonathan Latimer, *Sinners and Shrouds*; ▷John D. MacDonald, *Pale Gray for Guilt*.

PHOTOGRAPHY

▷George Harmon Coxe, *An Easy Way to Go*
▷Dick Francis, *Reflex*
  S. Ocork, *End of the Line*
  R. Ormerod, *Double Take*
  A.J. Quinnell, *Sharpshoot*
  Craig Rice, *The Thursday Turkey Murders*

POE, Edgar Allan • (1809–49)
US writer

Poe's crime stories (for example 'The Murders in the Rue

Read on
▶ Michael Harrison, *Murder in the Rue Royale*

Morgue', 'The Case of the Purloined Letter' and 'The Mystery of Marie Roget') are where detective fiction begins. They star the first amateur sleuth in fiction: Chevalier C. Auguste Dupin, a brilliant eccentric who solves mysteries by a blend of investigation and laser-like brain-power. The stories are narrated by a friend of Dupin's, slower-witted, dogged and full of admiration. Poe's horror stories may nowadays be better known, but in their day these crime tales influenced every detective writer from ▷Doyle to ▷Stout, from ▷Allingham to ▷Carr – and they still stand up today.

Poe's Dupin stories, with other tales such as 'The Gold Bug' are collected in *Tales of Mystery and Imagination*.

(stories about Dupin, as good as Poe's); ▷Arthur Conan Doyle, *The Adventures of Sherlock Holmes*; ▷G.K. Chesterton, *The Innocence of Father Brown*; ▷John Dickson Carr, *The Men Who Explained Miracles*.

POLICE PROCEDURALS

Ben Benson, *Target in Taffeta*
Rex Burns, *Angle of Attack*
Roger Busby, *Robbery Blue*
▷J.J. Marric, *Gideon's Day*
▷Ed McBain, *Hail, Hail, the Gang's All Here*
Maurice Procter, *The Midnight Plumber*
▷Dell Shannon, *Death of a Busybody*
Dorothy Simpson, *The Night She Died*
▷Maj Sjöwall and Per Wahlöö, *The Man on the Balcony*
Lawrence Treat, *Big Shot*
▷Hillary Waugh, *Last Seen Wearing . . .*
Colin Wilcox, *Doctor, Lawyer . . .*

POTTS, Jean • (born 1910)
US writer

Each Potts book shows us a close-knit community – family, village, small town – outwardly as placid as a saucer of milk, inwardly seething with frustration, misery and hatred. The more we find out about people, the more tension mounts, until it is released in an ending which surprises as much as it satisfies. No detectives are necessary in this twisted version of the American dream – the more folksy people are, the more certain we can be that they are nursing poisonous thoughts.

 Read on

• *Go, Lovely Rose; An Affair of the Heart.*
▶ ▷Helen McCloy, *Through a Glass Darkly*; ▷Andrew Coburn, *Goldilocks*; ▷Joseph Hansen, *The Man Everybody Was Afraid Of.*

THE DIEHARD (1956)

Lew Morgan is one of those crinkly-haired, big-smiling elderly men whom everyone adores. Or do they? He is the richest man in Turk Ridge, and everyone is beholden to him. As the book proceeds, every single one of Potts's characters discovers a reason for murdering him. Who will win the race, and how?

Potts's other books include *Blood Will Tell/Lightning Strikes Twice*, *The Footsteps on the Stairs*, *The Trash Stealer*, *The Little Lie*, *The Troublemaker* and *My Brother's Killer*.

POYER, Joe • (born 1939)
US writer

Poyer's first thriller, *Operation Malacca* (1968), has a brilliantly original basic idea. The US navy, anxious to neutralize an enemy H-bomb in the Straits of Malacca, recruits the scientist Dr Mortimer Keilty, who has worked out a way to communicate directly, in English, with dolphins. Keilty, in turn, recruits the dolphin Charlie. This simple idea lets Poyer reflect on the rights and wrongs of cold-war politics from an entirely unusual angle – that of an intelligent species quite different from our own – and it also lets him write magnificent underwater scenes, as Charlie swims into Top Security areas and through detection systems which no human could ever penetrate. The book reaches a shattering climax when the humans decide that the bomb must be destroyed – and that Charlie must be asked to sacrifice his own life to do so.

Poyer's other thrillers include *North Cape*, *The Balkan Assignment*, *The Chinese Agenda*, *Day of Reckoning*, *The Contract* and *Vengeance 10*.

PRICE, Anthony • (born 1928)
English writer

Price's thrillers are as complex and clever as ▷le Carré's, but faster-moving. Instead of paragraphs of leisurely reflection he writes brisk conversation, so that we must constantly sift several viewpoints to work out who can be trusted and who is suspect. His main interest is in how men (especially soldiers) react under threat, and his Intelligence officers are

 Read on

- *Tunnel War.*
- ▶ **Matching Poyer's questioning of the 'me right, you wrong' approach to international politics:** ▷Andrew Coburn, *Company Secrets.*
- ▶ **Picking up the 'alien species' theme:** James Blish, *A Case of Conscience* (science fiction).
- ▶ **Fast action, above and below the water:** Melville Ross, *Trigger.*

 Read on

- *A Prospect of Vengeance.*
- ▶ Thomas Gifford, *The Glendower Legacy*; ▷Bryan Forbes, *The Endless Game*; ▷Len Deighton, *Berlin Game*; ▷Duncan Kyle, *The King's Commissar.*

proud of their military backgrounds and despise those (like Oliver St John in several of the later books) who don't. The books' intermittently recurring cast of characters is led by David Audley, an intellectually brilliant, emotionally frigid man whose passion is military history. This leads Price to weave information about past campaigns into his stories, often making them keys to the whole plot. *Colonel Butler's Wolf*, for example, is set at Hadrian's Wall; *The Old Vengeful* draws on old naval battles (especially one from the Napoleonic Wars); *Sion Crossing* describes a modern espionage struggle on a site used in the American Civil War.

A NEW KIND OF WAR (1987)

The book begins in Greece in 1945, when young David Audley encounters two strangers on an ancient footpath. Audley knows the path from a history of the nineteenth-century Greek War of Independence, and memories of that war add zest to a fast-paced story about British Intelligence in post-war Germany.

Price's thrillers (each of which is set at a different stage of Audley's career) include *The Labyrinth Makers, October Men, Other Paths to Glory, Our Man in Camelot, The Hour of the Donkey, Soldier No More* and *For the Good of the State*.

PRIVATE EYES

Andrew Bergman, *The Big Kiss-off of 1944* (Jack LeVine)
▷Raymond Chandler, *Farewell, My Lovely* (Philip Marlowe)
Peter Corris *O'Fear* (Cliff Hardy)
▷Howard Engel, *A City Called July* (Benny Cooperman)
▷Loren D. Estleman, *Angel Eyes* (Amos Walker)
▷Dashiell Hammett, *The Maltese Falcon* (Sam Spade)
Michael Z. Lewin, *Ask the Right Question* (Albert Samson)
▷Ross Macdonald, *The Underground Man* (Lew Archer)
▷John Milne, *Dead Birds* (Jimmy Jenner)
▷Robert B. Parker, *The Godwulf Manuscript* (Spenser)
Roger L. Simon, *Peking Duck* (Moses Wine)
Ernest Tidyman, *Shaft* (John Shaft)
Jonathan Valin, *Natural Causes* (Harry Stoner)

Q

QUEEN, Ellery
US writer

'Ellery Queen' was the pseudonym of two cousins, Frederic Dannay (1905–82) and Manfred Lee (1905–71). 'Ellery Queen' is also the name of their detective. The cousins wrote novels, plays and short stories, and edited several crime-fiction weekly and monthly magazines including the *Ellery Queen Mystery Magazine*. Their stories are brilliant pot-boilers. Characterization and style take second place to plot, and to the careful planting of clues and red herrings, which distract the reader till the very last line. Typically, Ellery Queen's father, Inspector Richard Queen, is faced by an apparently insoluble murder, and calls on his son, the dandyish crime writer Ellery Queen, to help him find the guilty person. The formula was unvaried, except for locations and murder-methods, for 45 years, and produced some of the most reliably intriguing brain-teasers in the genre.

Queen's best novels were written before 1935 and after 1942 – in between the authors concentrated more on plays and on editing their magazine. 'Great' Queen novels include (from the early period) *The Greek Coffin Mystery*, *The Four of Hearts* (set in a believable Hollywood), and (from the later period) *Calamity Town*, *Ten Days' Wonder*, *The Finishing Stroke* and *A Fine and Private Place*. *The Case Book of Ellery Queen* is a good anthology of short stories. Under the name 'Barnaby Ross', the authors wrote a series of linked books featuring the actor-detective Drury Lane; the first is *The Tragedy of X*.

 Read on

▶ ▷George Harman Coxe, *Murder With Pictures*; ▷Francis Durbridge, *The Other Man*; ▷S.S. van Dine, *The Greene Murder Case*; James Holding, writing as 'Ellery Queen Junior', published several stories in the 1960s which are both splendid mysteries in their own right and spoofs of 'Ellery Queen': his detectives are based on the two (real life) authors of Ellery Queen. Good samples: 'The Hong Kong Jewel Mystery'; 'The Tahitian Powder Mystery'.

QUENTIN, Patrick • (born 1912)
US writer

'Patrick Quentin' is the pseudonym of Hugh Callingham
Wheeler, writing sometimes on his own, sometimes with
collaborators. His books are full of surprises and red
herrings, and many have a theatre or film background. His
best known detective is the Broadway theatre impresario
Pete Duluth. Under the name 'Q. Patrick', Wheeler and his
main collaborator Richard Wilson Webb wrote a second
series, starring the well-educated, compassionate New York
detective Lieutenant Timothy Trant. Under a third pseudonym, 'Jonathan Stagge', Wheeler and Webb wrote half a
dozen books starring the small-town doctor Hugh Westlake.

Quentin's Duluth books include *Puzzle for Players, Black
Widow/Fatal Woman* and *The Wife of Ronald Sheldon/My Son
the Murderer* (one of his finest stories, narrated by Duluth's
brother Jake, whose son is accused of murdering a playboy
publisher). Patrick's Trant books include *The Man With Two
Wives, Shadow of Guilt* and *Family Skeletons*. Stagge's
Westlake books include *The Dogs Do Bark/Murder Gone to
Earth, Funeral for Five/Turn of the Table* and *Death's Old Sweet
Song*. Quentin also wrote many stage plays, and the books
for the musicals *A Little Night Music, Candide, Pacific
Overtures* and *Sweeney Todd*.

Read on

▶ **To the Duluth books:**
  ▷Dashiell Hammett, *The
  Thin Man.*
▶ **To the Trant books:**
  Dorothy Hughes, *The
  Cross-Eyed Bear.*
▶ **To the Westlake books:**
  ▷Jean Potts, *The Diehard.*

R

RADLEY, Sheila • (born 1928)
English writer

'Sheila Radley' is the pseudonym of Sheila Robinson, who also writes non-fiction under her own name and Gothic romances as 'Hester Rowan'. Radley's detective stories are set in a small (and magnificently evoked) country town. The main characters, led by Chief Inspector Quantrill, recur from book to book, developing as the series proceeds. Quantrill solves his cases by a mixture of procedural routine and his knowledge of the human condition, but he is no super-sleuth, and makes all-too-human mistakes. Radley excels at showing relationships between the sexes: a happy marriage, for example, in *Who Saw Him Die?*, or Quantrill's infatuation for his (female) sergeant in *Fate Worse than Death*.

A TALENT FOR DESTRUCTION (1982)
The vicar of Breckham Market is domineering, attractive, and desperate that his shaky marriage to a faithful but unhappy wife should appear perfect in the eyes of his flock, even when he takes a mistress. This girl is manipulative, delighting in the havoc she raises. Then murder is committed – and the investigation puts further stress on the vicar and his wife. Throughout the book, their relationship is sensitively drawn.

 Read on

- *The Chief Inspector's Daughter.*
- ▷ Ruth Rendell, *Some Lie and Some Die*; ▷ John Buxton Hilton, *Death in Midwinter*; ▷ W.J. Burley, *Wycliffe and the Schoolgirls.*

RAILWAYS AND TIMETABLES

Lawrence G. Blochman, *Bombay Mail*
▷ Agatha Christie, *Murder on the Orient Express*
▷ Freeman Wills Crofts, *The 12.30 from Croydon*

▷Graham Greene, *Stamboul Train/Orient Express*
  M. Hinxman, *Corpse Now Arriving*
  C. Hyde, *Maxwell's Train*
▷H.R.F. Keating, *Inspector Ghote Goes By Train*
  Derek Lambert, *Golden Express*
  C. Leach, *Killing Frost*

RATHBONE, Julian • (born 1935)
English writer

As well as thrillers and detective stories, Rathbone has written 'literary' novels, including *King Fisher Lives* (about a US hippie trying to escape from materialist western society) and *Joseph* (set in Spain during the Peninsular War in 1810). His thrillers, very much in the tradition of ▷Eric Ambler, include two series, set respectively in Turkey and in Spain. The Turkish books, each self-contained, are linked by two recurring characters, the incorruptible, humane policeman Nur Arslan Bey and his corruptible chief Alp Vural Bey. A typical story is *Kill Cure* (1975), about a charity worker carrying medicines to Bangladesh who finds that someone has placed a deadly poison among her stock, a prize for both terrorists and the police. A typical book in the Spanish series is *Bloody Marvellous* (1975), in which a man is persuaded to smuggle drugs – and sets out to double-cross his employers. Rathbone's detective series, set in 'Brabt' (an imaginary state bordering Holland and Belgium) star Police Commissioner Jan Argand, who follows in the footsteps of ▷Freeling's Van der Valk.

Rathbone's other Turkish books are *Diamonds Bid*, *Hand Out*, *With My Knives I Know I'm Good* and *Trip Trap*. His other Spanish books include *Carnival!* and *A Raving Monarchist*, and his Argand books include *The Euro-Killers*, *Base Case* and *Watching the Detectives*.

 Read on

- *Lying in State*; *A Spy of the Old School.*
▶ **To Rathbone's thrillers:**
  ▷Eric Ambler, *The Mask of Dimitrios/Coffin for Dimitrios*; Michael Kenyon, *May You Die in Ireland*; ▷Julian Symons, *The Plot Against Roger Rider.*
▶ **To his detective novels:**
  ▷Nicolas Freeling, *Tsing-Boum.*

REAL PEOPLE OR EVENTS
(in fictional stories)

▷Simon Brett, *So Much Blood* (Mary, Queen of Scots)
  W.F. Buckley, *See You Later, Alligator* (Cuban missile crisis)

Don de Lillo, *Libra* (President Kennedy)
▷Frederick Forsyth, *The Day of the Jackal* (de Gaulle)
▷Hammond Innes, *The Last Voyage* (Captain Cook)
▷Bob Langley, *Conquistadores* (Falklands War)
Edward Marston, *The Merry Devils* (Elizabethan actors)
▷Josephine Tey, *The Daughter of Time* (Princes in the Tower)
▷Robert van Gulik, *The Chinese Maze Murders* (ancient Chinese judge)

REED, Eliot
see **AMBLER, Eric**

RELIGIOUS SLEUTHS

▷G.K. Chesterton, *The Innocence of Father Brown* (stories)
Andrew M. Greeley, *Angels of September* (Father Blackie Ryan)
▷Harry Kemelman, *Friday the Rabbi Slept Late* (Rabbi Small)
Charles Merrill Smith, *Reverend Randollph and the Fall from Grace, Inc* (Pastor Con Randollph)
▷Ellis Peters, *A Morbid Taste for Bones* (Brother Cadfael)
Joseph Telushkin, *The Final Analysis of Doctor Stark* (Rabbi Daniel Winter)

RENDELL, Ruth • (born 1930)
English writer

Rendell writes books of three entirely different kinds. Her Chief Inspector Wexford novels are atmospheric police procedurals, set in the towns and villages of prosperous, leafy Surrey. The stories depend greatly on the character of Wexford himself, a liberal and cultured man appalled at the psychological pressures which drive people to crime. Those pressures are the subject of Rendell's non-Wexford books published under her own name. They are stories of inadequacy, obsession and paranoia, told in a matter-of-fact style which enhances the unsettling effect of what Rendell has to say. The same intensity marks Rendell's third group of books, written under the pseudonym 'Barbara Vine'. They, too, show how remorseless psychological pressure leads to

 Read on

▶ **To the Wexford books:**
Elizabeth Lemarchand, *The Affacombe Affair*; ▷Sheila Radley, *Death and the Maiden*; S.T. Haymon, *Death of a God*.
▶ **To *The Face of Trespass*:**
Fay Weldon, *Puffball*; Joan Fleming, *Young Man I Think You're Dying*.
▶ **To Rendell's (and Vine's) psychological thrillers in general:**
▷Patricia Highsmith, *The Glass Cell*; Peter de

mental collapse and crime, but they concentrate less on individual character than on the relationships among groups of people: families, neighbours, chance acquaintances.

THE FACE OF TRESPASS (1974)
This typical non-Wexford novel focuses on Graham Lance-ton, a man who has tried to cut himself off from the pressures of life because he refuses to help his rich mistress murder her husband. Half-crazy, unsure of his own mental state, he visits France to see his dying mother – a trip which provokes the crisis he has spent the last six desperate months avoiding.

Rendell's Wexford books include *A New Lease of Death*, *Wolf To the Slaughter*, *A Guilty Thing Surprised*, *Some Lie and Some Die*, *A Sleeping Life* and *An Unkindness of Ravens*. Her psychological thrillers include *To Fear a Painted Devil*, *A Demon in My View*, *The Lake of Darkness*, *The Tree of Hands*, *Live Flesh*, *Talking to Strange Men* and *The Bridesmaid*. Her novels as 'Barbara Vine' are *A Dark-Adapted Eye*, *A Fatal Inversion*, *The House of Stairs* and *Gallowglass*. *Means of Evil* and *The Fever Tree* are collections of short stories.

ROSS, Barnaby
see QUEEN, Ellery

RUELL, Patrick
see HILL, Reginald

RYDER, Jonathan
see LUDLUM, Robert

Polnay, *The Price You Pay*; ▷ John Katzenbach, *The Traveller*.

S

SAYERS, Dorothy L(eigh) • (1893–1957)
English writer

Sayers' detective, Lord Peter Wimsey, is one of the giants of
the genre, a creation to match Holmes himself. Sayers' plots
are masterly, and all her settings (from Oxford college to East
Anglian village, from London advertising agency to the
House of Lords) are painstakingly researched. Sometimes her
1930s social attitudes grate – snobbishness and anti-
Bohemianism in particular – but her stories are ingenious,
her characters are fascinating and her planting of clues is
fair. Some readers prefer the books in which Wimsey courts
and marries Harriet Vane (a crime-writer not unlike Sayers
herself); others prefer the non-Vane books, uncluttered with
arch or witty repartee.

THE NINE TAILORS (1934)
The story effortlessly blends such ingredients as country
working-class morality, a flood, an unworldly vicar, an
emerald necklace, a peal of bells and skullduggery in
northern France. Wimsey is on peak form, and the book has
a wonderfully English atmosphere, compounded of wintry
weather, fen countryside and above all the brooding
churchyard and ancient bells of Fenchurch St Paul.

Sayers' books including Vane are *Strong Poison, Gaudy
Night, Have His Carcase* and *Busman's Honeymoon*. The non-
Vane Wimsey books are *Whose Body?, Clouds of Witness,
Unnatural Death/The Dawson Pedigree, The Unpleasantness at
the Bellona Club, The Five Red Herrings/Suspicious Characters,
Murder Must Advertise* and *The Nine Tailors. Lord Peter Views
the Body* and *Hangman's Holiday* are short-story collections.
(The 21 Wimsey stories are also collected, complete, in *Lord
Peter.*) Sayers wrote several non-Wimsey books with other

Read on

- *Strong Poison; Murder
  Must Advertise.*
▶ ▷Ngaio Marsh, *Enter a
  Murderer;* ▷Margery
  Allingham, *Police at the
  Funeral;* ▷S.S. Van Dine,
  *The Benson Murder
  Case;* ▷E.C. Bentley,
  Trent's Last Case.

people, notably the thriller in letter form *The Documents in the Case*.

SCHOOLS

▷Nicholas Blake, *A Question of Proof*
  Leo Bruce, *A Bone and a Hank of Hair*
  Stephen Cook, *Upperdown*
▷Amanda Cross, *The Theban Mysteries*
  Carolyn G. Hart, *The Rich Die Young*
▷John le Carré, *A Murder of Quality*
  Jill McGown, *Death of a Dancer*
  Jill Staynes and Margaret Storey, *A Knife at the Opera*

SCOTLAND

▷John Buchan, *Huntingtower*
▷Antonia Fraser, *The Wild Island*
  G. Hammond, *Adverse Report*
  Alan Hunter, *Gabrielle's Way*
▷Michael Innes, *Lament for a Maker*
▷Bob Langley, *Avenge the Belgrano*
  Frederic Lindsay, *Brond*
  M.R.D. Meek, *Split Second*
▷Gwen Moffat, *Snare*
▷Elizabeth Peters, *Legend in Green Velvet*
  Ian Rankin, *Knots and Crosses*
▷Mary Stewart, *Touch Not the Cat*
  Peter Turnbull, *Deep and Crisp and Even*

SHANNON, Dell
see LININGTON, Elizabeth

SHEPHERD, Michael
see LUDLUM, Robert

SHERMAN, Dan
US writer

Sherman writes not so much spy stories as stories about

 Read on

▶ ▷Len Deighton, *Berlin Game*; Derek Marlowe,

spies. He is fascinated by the psychological need some people have to define their own characters by loyalty or treachery. Most of his books are set in Europe, and have cold-war backgrounds, but exciting action is balanced against the interplay of personalities and the exploration of personal feelings and motives. In one book, *Dynasty of Spies* (1984), he invents an entire family who live by espionage, spanning the twentieth century from 1917 to the height of the cold war, serving on both sides, and painfully balancing family loyalties against those to state or political ideal.

Sherman's novels include *Riddle*, *The Mole*, *Swann*, *King Jaguar*, *The White Mandarin* and *The Prince of Berlin*.

A Dandy in Aspic; John Lear, *Death in Leningrad*.

SHERWOOD, John • (born 1913)
English writer

In the 1960s Sherwood wrote drily witty thrillers and 'classic' detective stories, of which the best known is *The Half Hunter* (1961), about a public schoolboy being initiated into real life in an off-season, murderous seaside resort. In the late 1970s, after several years' silence, Sherwood returned to crime writing and began a series starring green-fingered super-sleuth Celia Grant, who runs a nursery for rare plants. (Gardeners will find the background fascinating; non-gardeners will not find it intrusive.) Sherwood's early books include *Vote Against Poison*, *Undiplomatic Exit*, *Honesty Will Get You Nowhere* and *The Hour of the Hyenas*. His Celia Grant books include *Green Trigger Fingers*, *Flowers of Evil*, *A Botanist at Bay*, *Groves of Evil* and *The Mantrap Garden* (1986), in which Grant, trying to identify the vandalizer of a garden created by Gertrude Jekyll, becomes involved with an eccentric and highly-strung family with many dark secrets.

 Read on

- *The Limericks of Lachasse* (non-Grant); *A Bouquet of Thorns* (in which Grant's head gardener is accused of murder, her investigations lead to the discovery of past village scandals, and the whole community turns against her).
- ▶ **To Sherwood's non-Grant books:**
  ▷ Michael Gilbert, *The Long Journey Home*;
  ▷ Peter Dickinson, *Perfect Gallows*.
- ▶ **To his Grant books:**
  ▷ P.D. James, *An Unsuitable Job for a Woman*; Liza Cody, *Dupe*.

SHORT-STORY COLLECTIONS

▷ Ernest Bramah, *The Eyes of Max Carrados*
▷ G.K. Chesterton, *The Innocence of Father Brown*
▷ Carter Dickson, *The Department of Queer Complaints*
▷ Arthur Conan Doyle, *The Casebook of Sherlock Holmes*
▷ Stanley Ellin, *The Speciality of the House*

R. Austin Freeman, *The Singing Bone*
▷Celia Fremlin, *Don't Go to Sleep in the Dark*
Michael Harrison, *Murder in the Rue Royale*
▷Dorothy L. Sayers, *In the Teeth of the Evidence*

SHUTE, Nevil • (1899–1960)
English/Australian writer

Shute is known for war-stories (*What Happened to the Corbetts*, *Landfall*), and for such novels as *On The Beach*, set after the start of the nuclear holocaust. But he also wrote thrillers, in many of which ordinary people follow obsessions or live by their ideals despite all opposition from fellow human beings or hostile circumstances. Typical are *Pied Piper* (1942), in which an unassuming Englishman rescues several children from Nazi-occupied France, and *No Highway* (1948), in which an aircraft engineer, the only person in the world to know about metal fatigue, discovers that a passenger plane in which he is flying is likely to disintegrate in midair. In these books, as in all Shute's work, suspenseful action is balanced by sympathetic characterization, especially of the central figures.

Shute's other books include *So Disdained*, *The Rainbow and the Rose*, *Requiem for a Wren*, *An Old Captivity* and *In the Wet*.

 Read on

• *A Town Like Alice* (about a woman, marched across Malaya by Japanese captors in the second world war, who later sets about building a community in the Australian outback).
▶ Ernest K. Gann, *The High and the Mighty*; Paul Gallico, *The Poseidon Adventure*; Paul Theroux, *The Mosquito Coast*.

SIMENON, Georges • (1903–89)
Belgian writer

Simenon is best known for 84 crime stories featuring pipe-smoking, *calvados*-drinking Commissaire Maigret of the Paris police. The books are short, spare, and dense with local atmosphere. They concentrate on Maigret's investigations in bars, lodging houses and rain-soaked Paris streets, and on his casual-seeming, fatherly conversations with suspects and witnesses. As well as the Maigret books, Simenon wrote over 500 pulp books under a couple of dozen pseudonyms, and – under his own name – some 350 psychological thrillers: sinewy studies of people distracted by fear, obsession, despair or hate.

Simenon is one of the most consistent, as well as prolific, of authors. Each Maigret book is as good as the next; his thrillers are of equal quality – and rank with the work of the

 Read on

▶ **To Simenon's Maigret books:** ▷Nicholas Freeling, *Dressing of Diamond*; ▷James Melville, *The Wages of Zen*; ▷Trevanian, *The Main*.
▶ **To his non-Maigret novels:** ▷Julian Symons, *The Thirty-First of February*; ▷Graham Greene, *A Gun for Sale/This Gun for Hire*; ▷Patricia Highsmith, *Found in the Street*.

finest psychological novelists of the century: Camus, ▷Greene, Kafka. Good Maigret books to begin with are *Maigret's Pipe*, *Madame Maigret's Friend* or *Maigret Travels South*. Good thrillers to begin with are *The Man Who Watched the Trains Go By*, *Act of Passion* and *The President*.

SIMS, George • (born 1923)
English writer

Read on

- *Deadhand.*
- ▶ Cornelius Hirschberg, *Florentine Finish*; Jonathan Gash, *Firefly Gadroon*; Michael Delving, *Die Like a Man.*

Sims' books offer the usual pleasure of watching people doggedly solving ghastly, apparently inexplicable crimes. But they are crammed with other delights as well. Many are set among dealers in antiques, books and coins, and the detail of Sims' characters' professions is as fascinating as his plots. He brilliantly describes the underbelly of the London business world – dusty backstreet shops, pawnbrokers, auction rooms. And he writes fully-fleshed characters, allowing them to grow and develop as the books proceed. All this makes his novels a little rich for some people – cakes overstuffed with plums. But for those who like ruminative, discursive crime books, he is a treat.

THE LAST BEST FRIEND (1967)
While old-books dealer Ned Balfour is in bed with a girl in Corsica, someone in London makes his old friend Sam Weiss fall to his death from a tenth-floor window-ledge. Who? Why? This is what Balfour sets out to discover, against the wishes of some extremely nasty thugs.

Sims' books include *Sleep No More*, *The Sand Dollar*, *Hunters Point*, *The End of the Web* and *Rex Mundi*.

SJÖWALL, Maj (born 1935) and WAHLÖÖ, Per (1926–75)
Swedish writers

Read on

- ▶ ▷Joseph Wambaugh, *The Choirboys*; Janwillem van de Wetering, *Death of a Hawker*; James Barnett, *Head of the Force.*

Sjöwall and Wahlöö wrote police-procedural novels starring the Stockholm detective Martin Beck. The authors were political activists, and wanted to use detective fiction to show some of the defects and dangers of Swedish society. But this is less apparent to non-Swedish readers than the harshness of the stories, the tension of the investigations, and the believability of characters and atmosphere (especially Beck's family life, and the very Swedish mixture of banter and formality between him and his colleagues at the precinct). If Ingmar Bergman had made police-procedural films, they might have been like this.

The Beck novels are *Roseanna*, *The Man on the Balcony*, *The Man Who Went Up in Smoke*, *The Laughing Policeman*, *The Fire Engine That Disappeared*, *Murder at the Savoy*, *The Abominable Man*, *The Locked Room*, *Cop Killer* and *The Terrorist*.

SMALL TOWNS AND VILLAGES
(UK):

    Catherine Aird, *Slight Mourning*
▷Robert Barnard, *Disposal of the Living*
    Francis Beeding, *Death Walks in Eastrepps*
    John Bingham, *Brock*
▷Agatha Christie, *A Pocket Full of Rye*
▷Elizabeth Ferrars, *Alive and Dead*
▷Sheila Radley, *Fate Worse than Death*
▷John Sherwood, *A Bouquet of Thorns*
    June Thomson, *Not One of Us*
▷Colin Watson, *Coffin, Scarcely Used*
▷Margaret Yorke, *The Cost of Silence*

(USA):

▷Andrew Coburn, *Widow's Walk*
    K.C. Constantine, *The Rocksburg Railroad Murders*
    Hildegarde Dolson, *To Spite Her Face*
▷Howard Engel, *A City Called July*
    Stanton Forbes, *Grieve for the Past*
▷Joseph Hansen, *The Man Everybody Was Afraid Of*
▷Charlotte MacLeod, *Vane Pursuit*
▷Jean Potts, *The Diehard*
    Richard Martin Stern, *Cry Havoc*
▷Ross Thomas, *Briarpatch*

SMITH, Wilbur • (born 1933)
South African writer

Many of Smith's swaggering adventure novels are set in

 Read on

● *Shout at the Devil* (the story of lion-hunting,

SPECIAL SKILLS REQUIRED

South Africa. Their backgrounds are war, mining and jungle exploration; their heroes are free spirits, revelling in the lawlessness and vigour of frontier life. *A Time to Die* (1989) is typical. It tells how Sean Courtney, a white safari guide, agrees to lead his rich US clients across the border into Mozambique, where the daughter is promptly kidnapped by South African guerrillas who demand that Courtney help them to smash the Communists. The fast-moving, gritty adventure plot is interwoven with Courtney's (somewhat inaccurate) memories of the history of southern Africa, and especially of Great Zimbabwe, the huge medieval fortress town once claimed as the castle of the legendary Queen of Sheba.

Smith's other novels include *Gold Mine*, *A Sparrow Falls* and the 'Courtneys of Africa' trilogy: *The Burning Shore*, *Power of the Sword* and *Rage* (about the lifelong feud of two half brothers during the last turbulent century of South African affairs).

crocodile-wrestling, ivory-poaching Flynn O'Flynn, whose Robin Hood-like humiliations of the sadistic German commissioner Fleischer take a serious turn when war is declared – this is 1914 – and he falls into a German trap).

▶ ▷ Desmond Bagley, *Running Blind*; ▷ John Gardner, *The Secret Generations*; ▷ Hammond Innes, *Campbell's Kingdom*; H. Rider Haggard, *King Solomon's Mines*.

SPECIAL SKILLS REQUIRED
(heroes or heroines with unusual occupations or expertise)

▷ Edward Candy, *Bones of Contention* (paediatrics)
  Charles A. Goodrum, *Dead for a Penny/Carnage of the Realm* (numismatics)
  Cornelius Hirschberg, *Florentine Finish* (diamond-selling)
▷ Harry Kemelman, *Friday the Rabbi Slept Late* (religion)
▷ Elizabeth Peters, *The Curse of the Pharaohs* (archaeology)
▷ John Sherwood, *A Bouquet of Thorns* (horticulture)
  Neville Steed, *Tinplate* (selling toy cars)

SPILLANE, Mickey (Frank Morrison) • (born 1918)
US writer

Spillane's Mike Hammer books are fast-moving pulp private-eye adventures. They pit his hero against drugs barons, Mafia bosses, crooked policemen, card sharps, international spies and straightforward hoodlums. Hammer punches and shoots his way to a solution, fending off busty blondes at

 Read on

▶ **To the Hammer books:**
Bill S. Ballinger, *The Body in the Bed*; Carter Brown, *The Pornbroker*; Richard S. Prather, *Kill Him Twice.*

every turn. The Hammer books are fascist, macho, chauvinist – any censorious adjective you can think of. To those who enjoy them, they are also inexhaustibly exciting, outranking countless imitations. Spillane also wrote several books starring Tiger Mann, a secret agent modelled on James Bond.

The Hammer books include *I the Jury*, *My Gun is Quick*, *Kiss Me Deadly*, *The Twisted Thing* and *Survival . . .Zero!*. The Mann books include *Day of the Guns* and *The Death Dealers*. *The Erection Set* is Spillane's attempt to write a 'really dirty book'; *The Last Cop Out* is a magnificent Mafia thriller.

SPORT

▷Dick Francis, *Trial Run* (Olympics)
John Francome and James MacGregor, *Riding High* (horse racing)
▷Dan Kavanagh, *Putting the Boot In* (association football)
▷H.R.F. Keating, *A Rush on the Ultimate* (croquet)
▷Emma Lathen, *Murder with Icing* (ice hockey)
Sam Llewellyn, *Dead Reckoning* (yacht racing)
K. Miles, *Double Eagle* (golf)
Ilie Nastase, *Net* (lawn tennis)
A. Neilson, *Monza Protest* (motor racing)
William Rushton, *W.G. Grace's Last Case* (cricket)
Nancy Spain, *Murder in Play* (tennis)
Allen Synge, *Hunters of the Lost Ashes* (cricket)

STAGGE, Jonathan
see QUENTIN, Patrick

STARK, Richard ● (born 1933)
US novelist

'Richard Stark' is one of the pseudonyms of ▷Donald E. Westlake. He writes hardboiled, fast-action thrillers. There are two series. One stars the amoral, emotionless Parker, a professional thief and murderer, the other an unsuccessful actor who turns to theft, Alan Grofield. Both men plan complex heists, conning banks, big city institutions and the Mafia. The battle of wits in each book produces nail-biting

 Read on

► **To the Parker books:**
▷James M. Cain, *Double Indemnity*; ▷Patricia Highsmith, *The Talented Mr Ripley*; Colin Dunne, *Ratcatcher*.
► **To the Grofield books:**
▷John Godey, *Never Put Off Till Tomorrow What*

tension, enlivened in the Parker books by sudden, brutal violence.

Stark's Parker books include *Point Blank/The Hunter*, *The Rare Coin Score*, *The Dame*, *Slayground* and *The Outfit* (a particularly tense battle between Parker and the Mafia). His Grofield books include *The Damsel* and *Lemons Never Lie*. Both characters appear in several books, including *The Score*, *The Handle* and *Butcher's Moon*.

STEIN, Aaron Marc • (born 1906)
US writer

Stein has published over 100 novels, under three names. As 'George Bagby' he writes about long-suffering Inspector Schmidt of Manhattan's Homicide Squad. Schmidt suffers from ever-aching feet and, to add to his burdens, every case he tackles involves him with people whose lifestyle he deplores – gays, hippies, charismatic Christians. As 'Hampton Stone' Stein writes thrillers about two Manhattan district attorneys, Jeremiah X. Gibson and 'Mac'. Each book is set in a different New York milieu: boxing, the art world, the gay scene, fringe theatre, and so on. Under his own name, Stein has written two series, one starring the archaeologists Tim Mulligan and Elsie Mae Hunt, and the other starring the civil engineer Matt Erridge. Each book in each series is set in a different foreign location. The heroes are visiting for the innocent purposes of work, but find themselves being shot at, menaced, framed and generally made to feel unwelcome despite the picture-postcard settings (Venice, Bruges, Greece, the South of France) in which they find themselves.

Recommended Bagby titles: *Murder at the Piano*, *Dead on Arrival*, *Mugger's Day*. Recommended Stone titles: *The Corpse That Refused to Stay Dead*, *The Babe with the Twistable Arm*, *The Funniest Killer in Town*. Recommended Stein titles: *The Case of the Absent-Minded Professor*, *Frightened Amazon* (both Mulligan and Hunt), *The Bombing Run*, *The Cheating Butcher* (both Erridge).

STEWART, Mary • (born 1916)
English writer

In some writers' hands, the 'women's romantic thriller' can

You Can Kill Today; ▷Donald E. Westlake, *The Mercenaries/The Smashers*; ▷Simon Brett, *Shock to the System*.

 Read on

▶ **To Stein's books set in New York:** Joseph Harrington, *The Last Known Address*; Christopher Newman, *The Sixth Precinct*; ▷Emma Lathen, *Murder With Icing*.
▶ **To his books with foreign locations:** ▷Michael Avallone, *London Bloody London*; ▷Julian Rathbone, *A Raving Monarchist*.

 Read on

● *This Rough Magic*; *The Gabriel Hounds*.

be sugary rubbish. By contrast, Stewart's humour, her beady-eyed view of human honesty and her knack of getting into her characters' skin by the second page, make her books irresistible. Her thrillers are set in beautiful parts of the world – Northumberland, Austria, southern France, Crete, Skye, Greece. In each story, an innocent young woman is caught up in mysterious and threatening activities – and as she solves the mystery (which takes the rest of the book) she also falls in love. As well as thrillers, Stewart has also written a trilogy of historical novels (*The Crystal Cave*, *The Hollow Hills*, *The Last Enchantment*) about Merlin and King Arthur.

THE MOON-SPINNERS (1962)
On holiday in Crete, Nicola Ferris stumbles across an injured Englishman and his friend. They have fled after seeing a local murder, and are hiding in the mountains. When Nicola gets back to her hotel, she finds out who the murderers are – and the mystery, and the love affair which grows out of it, take over the rest of her stay in Crete.

Stewart's other thrillers include *Wildfire at Midnight*, *Madam Will You Talk?*, *Nine Coaches Waiting*, *My Brother Michael*, *Airs Above the Ground* and *Touch Not the Cat*.

STOUT, Rex • (1886–1975)
US writer

Stout's detective, Nero Wolfe, is a woman-hating eccentric who lives in a large, old house with his cook, gardener, books, 10,000 orchids and his assistant and 'leg man' Archie Goodwin, the narrator of the stories. Wolfe is a genius, but lazy and reluctant to leave the house. Archie is young, fond of excitement and high society living. He goes out for Wolfe, using his photographic memory to retail scenes and conversations to the great man in exact detail, so that deductions can be made and plans begun. The plots (almost always involving murder) are bizarre and complicated; the dialogue is witty; above all, the characters of Wolfe and Archie, and the twists and turns of their friendship, are intriguing and unpredictable.

To counter (entirely justified) accusations of misogyny in the Wolfe books, Stout wrote a book (*Crime on her Hands/The Hand in the Glove*) starring the wisecracking female sleuth Dol Bonner. Set in a high society 1930s mansion, full of

▶ M.M. Kaye, *Death in Zanzibar*; Margaret Carr, *Blindman's Bluff*.

 Read on

▶ Robert Goldsborough, *Death on Deadline* (excellent Stout imitation, using Wolfe, Goodwin and all the master's other characters and themes); ▷Lawrence Block, *The Topless Tulip Caper* (a spoof); ▷H.R.F. Keating, *A Rush on the Ultimate*; ▷Ellery Queen, *The Egyptian Cross Mystery*.

disagreeable people, it fizzes with energy, like the 'screwball comedies' Hollywood made in the good old days.

The Wolfe novels (over 40) begin with *Fer-de-Lance* (one of the best), and include *Where There's a Will, Might As Well Be Dead, The League of Frightened Men* (Stout's own favourite) and *Death of a Dude*.

STUART, Ian
see **MacLEAN**, Alistair

SYMONS, Julian • (born 1912)
English writer

 Read on

● *The End of Solomon Grundy.*
▶ Joan Fleming, *The Man from Nowhere*;
▷ Patricia Highsmith, *Ripley's Game*; ▷ Ruth Rendell, *The Face of Trespass.*

Symons is an important figure behind the scenes of English crime fiction: reviewing, encouraging, founding societies, editing anthologies, administering prizes, and writing one of the best surveys of the genre, *Bloody Murder/Mortal Consequences* (1972). He has published two dozen novels of his own: fiendishly complicated murder plots, often involving swindles or family betrayals going back over a generation, and told in a relaxed, throwaway style distinctly at odds with the sinister obsessions of his characters. Few writers tease their readers quite so thoroughly – if you like crime stories which are intellectual Chinese boxes, bursting with red herrings, Symons is for you.

THE PLOT AGAINST ROGER RYDER (1973)
Ryder, a self-made millionaire, hires a detective to show that his wife is having an affair with his oldest friend. Then he invites friend, wife, estranged daughter and the friend's son (who shares a flat with a policeman in the Fraud Squad) to a villa in Spain – and disappears. What happened? Who is plotting against whom? Is anything what it seems to be? The major clue stares you in the face throughout the book, and Symons' smoke screens are so brilliant that you can read it twice running and still be fooled.

Symons' other novels include *The Broken Penny, The Colour of Murder, The End of Solomon Grundy, The Man Whose Dreams Came True* and *The Man Who Lost His Wife*.

TARRANT, John
see EGLETON, Clive

TAYLOR, Andrew • (born 1951)
English writer

Taylor is best known for his crime capers starring William Dougal, an engaging young man whose ambition in life is to do the best he can – first for himself, then for others. His willingness to accept what fate offers each day leads him into adventure, crime and (often) farce. In each book he finds, and loses, a girlfriend. Taylor is good at comic set pieces, and brilliant at describing social embarrassment. He has also written two non-Dougal thrillers, *The Second Midnight* and *Blacklist*. These are house-of-mirrors, who's-doublecrossing-whom spy stories, like ▷le Carré's but in fast-forward mode.

CAROLINE MINISCULE (1982)
Dougal, blackmailed by his less scrupulous, more effective adversary Hanbury into using his knowledge of medieval manuscripts to help track down some diamonds, decides to look for the jewels on his own account. The book proceeds to a frantic chase, as he and his girlfriend Amanda try to keep one step ahead of Hanbury, to stay out of trouble, and to find the diamonds.

Taylor's Dougal books include *Waiting for the End of the World, Our Father's Lies, An Old School Tie* and *Freelance Death*.

 Read on

- *Waiting for the End of the World.*
▶ ▷Dan Kavanagh, *Fiddle City*; James Pattinson, *Dangerous Enchantment*; ▷John Godey, *The Reluctant Assassin/A Thrill a Minute With Jack Albany*; ▷Eric Ambler, *The Light of Day.*

TERRORISTS

John Burmeister, *The Weatherman Guy*
▷ Eric Clark, *Send in the Lions*
▷ Jon Cleary, *Dragons at the Party*
▷ Bob Cook, *Questions of Identity*
▷ John Crosby, *An Affair of Strangers*
Colin Dunne, *Hooligan*
▷ Palma Harcourt, *Limited Options*
▷ Geoffrey Jenkins, *In Harm's Way*
▷ John le Carré, *The Little Drummer Girl*
▷ Magdalen Nabb, *Prosecutor*
J. Patterson, *Black Market*
Conrad Voss Bark, *The Second Red Dragon*

TEY, Josephine • (1897–1952)
Scottish writer

'Josephine Tey' was a pseudonym of Elizabeth Mackintosh, who also wrote plays as 'Gordon Daviot'. Her five mystery novels starring urbane Inspector Grant include one of the best-known crime books ever written, *The Daughter of Time* (1951). In this Grant, laid up in hospital, uses modern criminological methods (and persuades reluctant visitors to do his legwork) to solve the mystery of the 1480s murder of the Princes in the Tower of London. Tey's other Grant novels, and her non-series books, are about twentieth-century crime. Her stories often involve abnormal psychology, and she is known for her understanding of human nature and for her meticulous background research – in *Miss Pym Disposes* (1946), for example, into a women's PE college.

THE FRANCHISE AFFAIR (1948)
Robert Blair, a country solicitor, is asked to represent Marion Sharpe who is accused of kidnapping, beating and imprisoning a young girl. The girl, Betty Kane, unerringly identifies the woman and the house, and Blair takes on the seemingly impossible task of showing that she is lying.

Tey's Grant books are *The Man in the Queue/Killer in the Crowd*, *A Shilling for Candles*, *To Love and Be Wise*, *The Daughter of Time* and *The Singing Sands*. Her non-series crime novels are *Miss Pym Disposes*, *The Franchise Affair* and *Brat Farrar*.

 Read on

• *The Singing Sands* (Grant); *Brat Farrar* (non-Grant).
▶ **To *The Franchise Affair*:** Nina Bawden, *The Odd Flamingo*.
▶ **To *Miss Pym Disposes*:** ▷ Gladys Mitchell, *Laurels are Poison*.
▶ **To Tey's work in general:** ▷ Francis Iles, *Malice Aforethought*; ▷ Margaret Millar, *A Stranger in My Grave*; ▷ Ngaio Marsh, *Spinsters in Jeopardy/The Bride of Death*.

THEATRE

▷Caryl Brahms and S.J. Simon, *A Bullet in the Ballet*
▷Simon Brett, *Star Trap*
  Elizabeth Daly, *The Book of the Dead*
  Clemence Dane and Helen Simpson, *Enter Sir John*
  Jane Dentinger, *Murder on Cue*
  Dulcie Gray, *No Quarter for a Star*
▷P.D. James, *The Skull Beneath the Skin*
▷Ngaio Marsh, *Vintage Murder*
  Edward Marston, *The Merry Devils*
  Ann Morice, *Death in the Round*
  Sara Woods, *Put Out the Light*

THOMAS, Craig ● (born 1942)
English writer

Thomas' cold-war action thrillers star Kenneth Aubrey, a trouble-shooter for British Intelligence. Aubrey's missions usually involve complex, top secret weaponry – disabling or stealing it if it is 'theirs', guarding it with his life if it is 'ours'. The books follow Aubrey's career chronologically, from his 'blooding' in *Rat Trap* (1976) to *The Bear's Tears* (1985), in which a long-prepared trap is sprung for British Intelligence, and unless Aubrey acts fast his own career, and the service in which he has spent his life, are doomed.

Thomas' novels include (in order) *Firefox, Wolfsbane, Snow Falcon, Sea Leopard, Jade Tiger* and *Firefox Down*. He also writes as 'David Grant' (*Moscow 5000, Emerald Decision*).

 Read on

● *The Fourth Durango.*
▶ Tony Williamson, *Doomsday Contract*;
  ▷Ted Allbeury, *The Secret Whispers*; ▷Clive Egleton, *Picture of the Year*; ▷John Trenhaile, *A View from the Square.*

THOMAS, Ross ● (born 1926)
US writer

Thomas' crime novels are as cynical as ▷Chandler's about the way US affairs are run. Every police officer, newspaper reporter, politician and lawyer is on the take, and there is little difference between business tycoons and crooks – the bigger they are, the worse they are. In this murky world Thomas' heroes move warily, taking pains to cover their backs, solving the mysteries, getting the girls, but usually affecting the rottenness of the system as little as a pebble thrown into churning sea. If all this were serious, it would be

 Read on

● *Chinaman's Chance; The Mordida Man.*
▶ Stephen Greenleaf, *Fatal Obsession*; ▷John D. MacDonald, *Pale Gray for Guilt*; ▷Robert B. Parker, *God Save the Child*; ▷George V. Higgins, *Outlaws.*

unbearably heavy. But Thomas writes in beautifully or-
ganized, wry prose, full of one-liners and acidly funny –
another quality he shares with Chandler.

BRIARPATCH (1984)

Who blew up Ben Dill's policewoman sister, and where had
she been getting all her money from? In answering these
questions, Dill takes the lid off his home city, somewhere in
the South, and finds not only the writhing maggots of local
politics but some very sleazy links with Washington and
with international crime.

Thomas' books include *The Singapore Wink*, *The Money
Harvest*, *If You Can't Be Good*, *The Eighth Dwarf* and
Missionary Stew. Under the name 'Oliver Bleeck' he has
written a series of similar thrillers starring Philip St Ives, a
professional arbitrator and trouble shooter. They include *The
Brass Go-Between*, *The Highbinders* and *No Questions Asked*.

TORRIE, Malcolm

see **MITCHELL, Gladys**

TOUGH GUYS AND GALS

▷Michael Avallone, *The Case of the Violent Virgin*
  Robert Crais, *The Monkey's Raincoat*
  Sue Grafton, *'A' is for Alibi*
▷Dan Kavanagh, *Duffy*
  Stephen Marlowe, *Trouble is My Name*
  Harold Q. Masur, *Bury Me Deep*
▷Mickey Spillane, *Kiss Me Deadly*
▷Richard Stark, *Point Blank/The Hunter*

TRAVEN, B(en) ● (1890–1969)

European/US writer

'B. Traven' was the pseudonym of a German (or possibly
Polish or Norwegian) immigrant to the USA, who published
half a dozen action thrillers in the 1920s–30s, and later won
fame when one of them, *Treasure of the Sierra Madre*, was
filmed with Humphrey Bogart. He boosted his reputation by

 Read on

▶ Joseph Conrad, *The
  Secret Agent*;
▷Hammond Innes,
  Campbell's Kingdom;
▷Desmond Bagley,
  Juggernaut.

refusing ever to appear in public, by claiming that he was his own translator (and that the real 'Traven' had mysteriously disappeared), and by allowing wild speculation about his identity, only resolved when he gave his first press interview in 1966, at the age of 76 – or 84, if, as he claimed, he was really born in 1882. His books are like Joseph Conrad's, combining muscular action with complex psychological investigation of men under stress, and philosophical reflection on the reasons (usually greed, ambition or ruthlessness) which caused their dilemmas in the first place. In *Treasure of the Sierra Madre* (1935), for example, a trio of crooked inadequates looks for gold in bandit country in the hills – a quest which ends in betrayal, violence and death.

Traven's other novels include *The White Rose*, *The Death Ship*, *The Bridge in the Jungle* and *The Rebellion of the Hanged*. *The Bandit Doctor* and *The Night Visitor* are collections of short stories.

TRENHAILE, John
English writer

Trenhaile's action-packed thrillers are complex stories of business, politics and family life, further tangled by the involvement of international Intelligence services. He is excellent at describing personal feelings, especially emotional pain, and writes well of the rights and duties of friendship and family. His books can be read separately, but the best known (all from the 1980s) also form two trilogies. *A Man Called Kyril*, *A View from the Square* and *Nocturne for the General* centre on General Povin and the internal politics of the KGB. *The Mahjong Spies*, *The Gates of Exquisite View* and *The Scroll of Benevolence* are about Chinese, Russian and British spies and financiers working for dominance in Hong Kong before it is returned to the Chinese People's Republic in 1997.

THE MAHJONG SPIES (1986)
Simon Young, managing director of a large Hong Kong business firm, becomes involved in a tussle between Russian and Chinese Intelligence services attempting to sabotage each other's chances of controlling future financial activity in the City. His Chinese-born wife and his children become involved, making political and financial scheming impinge on ordinary life in a moving and desperate way.

 Read on

▶ **To Trenhaile's Russian trilogy:** ▷Clive Egleton, *Troika*.
▶ **To his Hong Kong trilogy:** ▷Richard Condon, *Money is Love*.
▶ **To his books in general:** Nicholas Luard, *The Travelling Horseman*; ▷Bryan Forbes, *The Endless Game*.

TREVANIAN • (born 1925)
US writer

'Trevanian' is the pseudonym of Rodney Whitaker. Although he has written books of several kinds (including a 'literary' novel, *Katya*), he is best known for two thrillers, *The Eiger Sanction* and *The Loo Sanction*. They star Jonathan Hemlock, an art-collector who works as an assassin to finance his hobby. Hemlock is a sexual stud and has no emotional or moral feelings whatsoever. Some critics say that these novels are the ultimate in James Bond spoofs, with Trevanian's tongue firmly in his cheek. Others take them seriously. Whatever the case, the books (and *Shibumi*, also about an assassin – are none of us safe in our beds?) are full of action-crammed, breath-taking excitement. The climax of *The Eiger Sanction*, on the North face of the Eiger, is unputdownable.

THE MAIN (1976)
The Main is Montreal's immigrant quarter, home of people who have not yet made their way in society (that is, out of the Main) and others who have been forced to move back in. In this swarming underclass, Lieutenant LaPointe is investigating the death of young Tony Green. Until the dazzling revelation of who the killer is, our interest is less in the crime than in the life, character and working methods of LaPointe himself. Trevanian's evocation of place is rawly realistic, and the feeling of police work in a dangerous, edgy community is absolutely caught.

TREVOR, Elleston • (born 1920)
English writer

Under eight pseudonyms, Trevor has written over 100 works – children's novels, plays, non-fiction and thrillers. He is best known for adventure novels (often involving flying) published under his own name (*The Burning Shore/The Pasang Run*, *The Flight of the Phoenix*, *The Theta Syndrome*), and for a series of thrillers starring the extra-special British agent Quiller. These, written under the pseudonym 'Adam Hall', are fast-moving, world-wide adventures, violent, detailed and full of nailbiting tension. In *The Tango Briefing* (1973), for example, Quiller parachutes into the Sahara to blow up a cargo of secret nerve gas in a crashed plane before the Libyan secret police catch up with him.

Read on

▶ **To *The Main*:** ▷Georges Simenon, *Maigret and the Dosser/Maigret and the Bum*; ▷Chester Himes, *Blind Man With a Pistol/Hot Day, Hot Night*.

▶ **To Trevanian's thrillers:** ▷Joe Gores, *Come Morning*; ▷Bob Langley, *Traverse of the Gods*; ▷Jon Cleary, *The Pulse of Danger*.

Read on

▶ **To Trevor's flying adventures:** ▷Gavin Lyall, *Judas Country*; ▷Duncan Kyle, *Stalking Point*.

▶ **To Hall's Quiller books:** ▷Ian Fleming, *You Only Live Twice*; Donald Hamilton, *The Terminators*.

Other Quiller books include *The Berlin Memorandum/The Quiller Memorandum*, *The 9th Directive*, *The Kobra Manifesto* and *The Scorpion Signal*.

TV AND FILMS

▷Robert Bloch, *The Star Stalker*
▷Simon Brett, *A Series of Murders*
▷H.R.F. Keating, *Filmi, Filmi, Inspector Ghote*
  Charles Larson, *Muir's Blood*
  Jonathan Latimer, *Black is the Fashion for Dying*
  Nancy Livingstone, *Death in Close-up*
▷Patricia Moyes, *Falling Star*
  Maureen O'Brien, *Close Up On Death*
  Lawrence Sanders, *The Heirloom*
  Michael Tolkin, *The Player*
▷Donald E. Westlake, *Who Stole Sassi Manoon?*

U

UNDERWOOD, Michael • (born 1916)

English writer

'Michael Underwood' is the pseudonym of John Michael
Evelyn, a retired barrister. His 40 crime stories are both
police procedurals and law procedurals; that is, he shows us
first the sleuthing which lands the criminal in court, and
then the legal proceedings leading up to and climaxing in the
trial. His 'backstage' scenes of solicitors, barristers and
judges are magnificent, and he treats his readers with
fairness; we discover the clues in tandem with his detectives,
then we see the case being built up, and presented, step by
step. Typical books are *Murder on Trial*, *Death on Remand*, *The
Case Against Philip Quest*, *Rosa's Dilemma*, *Smooth Justice*,
Anything but the Truth, *Victim of Circumstance*, *A Compelling
Case* and *The Injudicious Judge* (1987), in which sarcastic Judge
Kilby, a terror to anyone who enters her court, is murdered,
the chief suspect is a barrister she has humiliated and the
sleuth is the instructing solicitor, Rosa Epton.

Read on

● *The Unprofessional Spy*
(Epton).
▶ ▷Sara Woods, *The Case is
Altered*; Henry Cecil, *A
Woman Named Anne*.

UNUSUAL LOCATIONS

Gavin Black, *A Dragon for Christmas* (Red China)
Suzanne Blanc, *The Green Stone* (Mexico)
Robert L. Fish, *Isle of the Snakes* (tropical jungle)
▷Duncan Kyle, *The Honey Ant* (Australian desert)
▷Gwen Moffat, *Last Chance Country* (Arizona desert)
John Morris, *Fever Grass* (Jamaica)
Michael Pearce, *The Mamur Zapt and the Night of the Dog*
(Cairo, 1910)
▷Julian Rathbone, *Diamonds Bid* (Turkey)

Masako Togawa, *Lady Killer* (Tokyo)
▷Arthur Upfield, *The Mystery of Swordfish Reef* (shark-fishing in Tasman Sea)
▷Robert van Gulik, *The Chinese Maze Murders* (eighth-century China)
Andrew York, *Tallant for Trouble* (Caribbean)

UPFIELD, Arthur • (1888–1964)
Australian writer

Upfield's books star Inspector Napoleon Bonaparte of the North Queensland Police. Bonaparte is half white, half Aborigine, and has been educated by both groups. On the one hand he has an MA from Brisbane University, with all the Old World cultural knowledge that suggests; on the other he is initiated in Aboriginal beliefs, customs and skills. He uses all this knowledge, coupled with a manner which combines spiky vanity (especially towards superiors) and charm, to solve crimes in every conceivable Australian location, from outback sheepstation to bustling city. Upfield was especially good at describing the bleak beauty of Australia's interior, and his books, unusually for their period, were liberal in their attitude to race, treating all people as of equal weight. This, allied to Bony's Holmesian ability to make deductions from the smallest and least likely clues, makes the 29 Bonaparte books as enjoyable as they are unusual.

THE CAKE IN THE HAT BOX (1955)
On a road not far from the Breen cattle station, Constable Stenhouse has been shot dead, and his Aborigine tracker has disappeared. Bonaparte takes up the case – and finds himself racing to a solution with the local Aborigines, who are also tracking the culprit down.

Other Bonaparte books include *No Footprints in the Bush*, *Death of a Swagman*, *Man of Two Tribes*, *Bony Buys a Woman* and *The Will of the Tribe*.

 Read on

- *Venom House*; *The Bone is Pointed*.
- ▷Tony Hillerman, *The Dark Wind*; ▷Peter Dickinson, *Skin Deep/The Glass Sided Ants' Nest*; ▷Duncan Kyle, *The Honey Ant* (thriller).

V

VAN DINE, S.S. • (1888–1939)
US writer

'S.S. Van Dine' was the pseudonym of Willard Huntington Wright. He was a founding father of US detective fiction, and his 12 Philo Vance books are classics. Vance is a 1920s man about town, an art critic, fond of his own voice and stupendously over-educated. In each book he pours out torrents of views on Beowulf, Ibsen, Tang China, Moselle wine, Egyptian scarabs – anything which the situation, or his passing whim, suggests to him. But if Vance himself is a pain, the mysteries are not. Van Dine was a stickler for the rules, insisting that detective stories should be fair intellectual games, with no cheating between writer and reader. His books are an addict's delight.

The Philo Vance books are *The Benson Murder Case, The Canary Murder Case, The Greene Murder Case, The Bishop Murder Case, The Scarab Murder Case, The Kennel Murder Case, The Dragon Murder Case, The Casino Murder Case, The Garden Murder Case, The Kidnap Murder Case, The Gracie Allen Murder Case/The Smell of Murder* and *The Winter Murder Case.*

 Read on

► ▷E.C. Bentley, *Trent's Last Case/The Woman in Black*; H.C. Bailey, *The Bishop's Crime*; ▷Ellery Queen, *The Egyptian Cross Mystery.*

VAN GREENAWAY, Peter
English writer

Van Greenaway's books are a teasing mixture of crime, thriller and philosophical fantasy. His style is joky and personal, full of asides and comments to the reader, and his characters and themes are a mixture of the everyday and the wildly bizarre. It is dream-country, and none the less thrilling or intriguing for that. Typical books are *'Cassandra' Bell* (1981), in which the prophecies of a deranged nineteenth-

Read on

► ▷George Sims, *Rex Mundi*; ▷Jon Manchip White, *The Garden Game*; Douglas Adams, *Dirk Gently's Holistic Detective Agency.*

century seer begin to come alarmingly true a century later, and *Mutants* (1986), in which Britain is devilishly plagued (and despite appearances, this book is truly chilling) by a race of mutant mice. Van Greenaway's other novels include *The Medusa Touch*, *Suffer! Little Children*, *Edgar Allan Who – ?*, *Graffiti* and *The Immortal Coil*.

VAN GULIK, Robert • (1910–67)
Dutch writer

Van Gulik's books are set in eighth-century China, and each describes several interlinked cases solved by the Chinese statesman Judge Dee. Dee was a real person, but van Gulik's stories are imaginary. The mysteries are unusual, and the detail of Chinese life is intriguing. Typical titles are *The Chinese Maze Murders*, *The Chinese Gold Murders*, *The Chinese Lake Murders* and *The Chinese Nail Murders*.

VIDAL, Gore • (born 1925)
US writer

Under his own name, Vidal has published one magnificent thriller, *Kalki*, about a deranged Vietnam veteran who imagines himself the reincarnation of the Hindu death-god and engineers the end of the world. Under the pseudonym 'Edgar Box' he has written three satirical, spoof murder mysteries starring the 1950s yuppie Peter Cutler Sargeant: *Death in the Fifth Position* is set in a ballet company; *Death Before Bedtime* is merciless about presidential politics; *Death Likes it Hot* involves murder at an exclusive Long Island houseparty.

VINE, Barbara
see RENDELL, Ruth

    Read on

▶ **To the mysteries:**
  ▷ Carter Dickson, *The Department of Queer Compaints* (short stories).
▶ **To the Chinese setting:**
  ▷ Ernest Bramah, *Kai Lung's Golden Hours*.

    Read on

▶ **To *Kalki*:** ▷ Richard Condon, *The Manchurian Candidate*; ▷ Jon Manchip White, *The Garden Game*.
▶ **To the books by 'Box':** ▷ H.R.F. Keating, *Death of a Fat God*; ▷ Charlotte MacLeod, *God Rest Ye Merry*.

W

WAINWRIGHT, John • (born 1921)
English writer

Wainwright worked for 20 years as a policeman, and is best known for gritty police procedurals set among the hills and moors of his native Yorkshire (*Evil Intent; The Worms Must Wait, Freeze Thy Blood Less Coldly, The Last Buccaneer*). But he is also known for international thrillers (*Prynter's Devil, Cause for a Killing*), and for violent psychological thrillers in a direct line from ▷B. Traven and ▷Patricia Highsmith. In *The Bastard* (1976), for example (one of the most nailbiting), a criminal and a policeman who hate each other are snowed up in a remote cottage high on the Yorkshire moors. One is hunter and one is hunted – but which is which?

 Read on

- *Who Goes Next?*
- ▶ **To Wainwright's police procedurals:** Peter Turnbull, *Deep and Crisp and Even*; ▷Reginald Hill, *Child's Play*.
- ▶ **To his psychological thrillers:** ▷Geoffrey Household, *Watcher in the Shadows*; Ivan Ruff, *Blood Country*.

WALLACE, Edgar • (1875–1932)
English writer

Wallace's fertile mind and busy pen produced over 100 novels, 60 books of short stories, 50 plays and a dozen volumes of journalism. He was a hack of genius, and his best work (for example the short stories in *The Mind of Mr J.G. Reeder/The Murder Book of Mr J.G. Reeder*, about a private detective solving locked-room and other mysteries for the Prosecution Service) rival ▷Doyle's for both ingenuity and atmosphere. His novels – atmospheric, melodramatic crime thrillers – set the style for a million black and white 'B' films, and now seem dated simply because so many people have imitated them. But his short stories are still magnificent.

Wallace's Reeder short-story collections include *Red Aces* and *The Guv'nor/Mr Reeder Returns*. Other excellent collections are *The Law of the Four Just Men/Again the Three Just Men* and

 Read on

- ▶ **To Wallace's Reeder stories:** ▷G.K. Chesterton, *The Club of Queer Trades*; H.C. Bailey, *Call Reggie Fortune*; R. Austin Freeman, *The Singing Bone*; Isaac Asimov, *Tales of the Black Widowers*.
- ▶ **To his crime thrillers:** E. Phillips Oppenheim, *The Grassleyes Mystery*.
- ▶ **To his locked-room mysteries:** ▷Carter Dickson, *The Ten Teacups*.

Again the Ringer. Good anthologies are *Forty-Eight Short Stories*, *The Stretelli Case* and *Nig-Nog*. Worthwhile novels include *The Four Just Men*, *Kate Plus Ten*, *The Angel of Terror/The Destroying Angel*, *Room Thirteen* and the splendid locked-room mystery *The Door With Seven Locks*.

WAMBAUGH, Joseph ● (born 1937)
US writer

A former Los Angeles police sergeant, Wambaugh has written straight novels about police work and its psychological effects – *The New Centurions* and *The Blue Knight*. But he is better known for black-farce police procedurals such as *The Onion Field* (1974), *The Choirboys* (1976), *The Black Marble* (1978) and *The Glitter Dome* (1981). These show rape, drugs, extortion, mugging and murder as if they were the normal ingredients of life, and Wambaugh's cops react with a surrealist humour similar to the wisecracking in Joseph Heller's war novel *Catch-22* or the (softer-centred) TV series *M∗A∗S∗H*.

 Read on

● *The Secrets of Harry Bright*; *Echoes in the Darkness*.
▶ ▷Chester Himes, *Blind Man With a Pistol/Hot Day, Hot Night*; James Barnett, *Head of the Force*; Rex Burns, *The Alvarez Journal*; ▷Trevanian, *The Main*.

WAR STORIES

▷Pierre Boulle, *Bridge on the River Kwai*
  Brian Callinson, *Trapp's War*
▷Len Deighton, *Bomber*
  Emma Drummond, *Forget the Glory*
▷Colin Forbes, *The Palermo Ambush*
▷C.S. Forester, *The Gun*
▷Alistair MacLean, *The Guns of Navarone*
  Nicholas Monsarrat, *The Cruel Sea*
  Denis Wheatley, *The Black Baroness*

WATSON, Colin ● (1920–83)
English writer

Watson's invented Flaxborough, deep in the English fens, is a trim, prosperous market town. Behind its net-curtained bow windows and in the back premises of its olde-worlde shops unspeakable things are happening – and it is for Inspector Purbright and cherubic-faced Sergeant Love to root them out. The Flaxborough novels blend social satire with

 Read on

▶ ▷Pamela Branch, *Lion in the Cellar*; Jonathan Gash, *The Tartan Ringers*; Joyce Porter, *Dover Three*; ▷Robert Barnard, *Bodies*.

spectacularly macabre crimes, a mixture as satisfying as it is unusual.

The Flaxborough novels include *Coffin, Scarcely Used, Lonelyheart 4122, Broomsticks Over Flaxborough/Kissing Covens, The Naked Nuns/Six Nuns and a Shotgun* and *One Man's Meat/It Shouldn't Happen to a Dog*. Apart from his novels, Watson is also known for a witty history of the 'golden age' of English crime fiction, *Snobbery With Violence*.

WAUGH, Hillary • (born 1920)
US writer

Waugh published some books under the pseudonyms 'Harry Walker' and 'H. Baldwin Taylor', but they have since been reissued under his own name. He also writes big-old-house Gothic stories as 'Elissa Grandower' (*Seaview Manor, The Secret Room of Morgate House*). His non-series novels include *Last Seen Wearing . . .* (1953), a police-procedural in which the search for a lost college girl is told from four separate points of view, and *Parrish for the Defence/Doctor on Trial* (1974), in which the character of Parrish himself, a vain, oversexed but brilliant trial lawyer, is as vital to the story as the trial in which he takes part. Waugh is best known for two police-procedural series. The Fellows books are set in a small Connecticut town, whose respectable-seeming citizens have the standard small-town zest for corruption, mayhem and murder, crimes investigated by sleepy-seeming but worldly-wise Chief Fellows. The Sessions books are harder-boiled murder mysteries set in Manhattan and involving Detective Frank Sessions of Homicide.

Waugh's Fellows books include *Jigsaw/Sleep Long My Love, Prisoner's Plea* and *The Con Game*. His Sessions books include *'30' Manhattan East, The Young Prey* and *Finish Me Off*. His private-eye novels include *Hope to Die, The Odds Run Out* and *The Glenna Powers Case*.

WELCOME, John • (born 1914)
Irish writer

As well as thrillers, Welcome has written several non-fiction books about jockeys and horse-racing, and has edited anthologies of crime, racing and espionage stories. His

 Read on

▶ **To Waugh's Fellows books:** ▷ Jean Potts, *Go, Lovely Rose*; ▷ Andrew Coburn, *Goldilocks*.
▶ **To his Sessions books:** Rex Burns, *The Alvarez Journal*; Ruth Fenisong, *Miscast for Murder*.

 Read on

▶ ▷ Eric Ambler, *A Kind of Anger*; ▷ David Dodge, *Angel's Ransom*; Paula Gosling, *A Running Duck*;

novels are chase-thrillers, involving fast action in glamorous or unusual places. *A Painted Devil* (1988) is typical. Mike Ashley, a young solicitor, is investigating a girl's claims to an inheritance. She disappears, and he sets out to find her – a chase which takes him to Ireland, Italy, Egypt, the haunts of shady London antique dealers and even shadier race-track promoters, and ends with a shattering climax in a lonely house in the Welsh hills. The style is laconic, the pace breathless and the action never flags.

Welcome's other thrillers are *Run for Cover*, *Stop at Nothing*, *Wanted for Killing*, *Go for Broke*, *Grand National* and *Bellary Bay*.

▷Duncan Kyle, *The Dancing Men.*

WESTLAKE, Donald E(dwin) • (born 1933)
US writer

Westlake also uses the pseudonyms ▷'Richard Stark' and ▷'Tucker Coe'. Under his own name, he began by writing serious suspense novels, but with *The Fugitive Pigeon* (1965) he began the kind of books for which he is best known: comedy thrillers, among the funniest in the business. Many (e.g. *The Hot Rock*, *Bank Shot*, *Jimmy the Kid*, *Help! I Am Being Held Prisoner*, *Good Behaviour*) star a gang of incompetent crooks led by the indolent, ever optimistic Dortmunder. Westlake's other heroes range from a conman in 1860s San Francisco (in *Gangway!*, written with ▷Brian Garfield) to the bushy-tailed Mafioso of *The Busy Body* (1966), forced to exhume a body on which half a million dollars' worth of heroin has been hidden – only to have the body stolen from under his nose, the start of a 'chase comedy' as breathless and preposterous as any silent film.

Westlake's early, serious thrillers are *The Mercenaries/The Smashers*, *Killing Time/The Operator*, *361*, *Killy* and *Pity Him Afterwards*. His farces include *Spy in the Ointment*, *Who Stole Sassi Manoon?*, *Two Much!*, *Brothers Keepers*, *A New York Dance/Dancing Aztecs*, *Nobody's Perfect* and *Trust Me On This*.

 Read on

▶ ▷Lawrence Block, *The Burglar in the Closet*; ▷John Godey, *Never Put Off Till Tomorrow What You Can Kill Today*; Tony Kenrick, *Two for the Price of One.*

WHITE, Jon Manchip • (born 1924)
Welsh writer

White has written travel and history books, poetry and a dozen novels and 'extravagant tales'. In the 'tales', White

 Read on

▶ ▷Duncan Kyle, *Black Camelot*; Kate Wilhelm, *Smart House*; C.S. Lewis, *That Hideous Strength.*

plunges his heroes into utterly unlikely situations and adventures, which he then tells with deadpan seriousness, in the way of dreams. In *Nightclimber* the hero has to climb not only mountains but high buildings to outwit the villains and win the game. In *The Game of Troy* an insane millionaire hunts his wife and her architect lover through a vast maze designed by the architect and booby-trapped by the millionaire. In *The Garden Game* mercenaries fall into the hands of a group of rich men who relax by watching fights to the death along the lines of ancient Roman gladiatorial contests. Many people have written surrealist, dream-like books and action thrillers, but outside science fiction, White is the only author to combine the two.

White's other thrillers include *Send for Mr Robinson* and *The Moscow Papers*. His novels include *Mask of Dust, Hour of the Rat* and *The Rose in the Brandy Glass*.

WRIGHT, Eric
Canadian writer

Wright's books star Inspector Charlie Salter of the Toronto Police. Each novel traces a single enquiry, but the series also gives a rounded picture of Salter himself, the ups and downs of his career, his marriage and his family life. As a policeman, Salter's main advantage is his sympathetic understanding for people of all kinds (except his superiors, with whom he is often at loggerheads). Wright's supporting characters are an exotic mix, and his locations (for example singles bars and lonelyhearts clubs in *A Single Death*) are evoked with a richness of detail which – in true 'classic' style – distracts attention from carefully-planted clues. His books include *The Night the Gods Smiled, A Body Surrounded by Water, Death in the Old Country* and *Smoke Detector*.

A QUESTION OF MURDER (1988)
At a time when most of the Toronto police are concerned with protecting a visiting princess, Salter is detailed to investigate a bombing. It looks as though Danny Pearson has been blown up during a 'war' between shop owners and street traders in a fashionable tourist area. But Salter uncovers other motives, other murderous intrigues.

 Read on

- *A Single Death; A Sensitive Case.*
- ▶ **To the police work:**
  ▷Sheila Radley, *Fate Worse than Death*; W.J. Burley, *Wycliffe and the Schoolgirls.*
- ▶ **To the Canadian setting:** ▷Trevanian, *The Main*; ▷Howard Engel, *A City Called July.*

Y

YORK, Jeremy
see CREASEY, John

YORKE, Margaret • (born 1924)
English writer

'Margaret Yorke' is the pseudonym of Margaret Nicholson. Her first few books were detective stories (*Silent Witness, Grave Matters, Cast for Death*) starring Patrick Grant, but in the 1970s she began writing the psychological suspense thrillers for which she is best known. She has an unnerving ability to escalate the fears and tensions of ordinary lives, and often shows us several apparently normal, apparently unconnected people who become enmeshed by the commission or effects of some ghastly crime. Her style is plain, even throwaway, but her vision that natural justice always prevails and her evocation of the thought-processes of her characters (especially young women) make her books unique. They include *The Point of Murder, Death on Account, The Smooth Face of Evil, Intimate Kill* and *Crime in Question*.

SPEAK FOR THE DEAD (1988)
A grocer hires an ex-policeman to locate Gordon Matthews, the man who was married to, and killed, his daughter Anne. Matthews has served his sentence and re-married. But now the enquiry triggers a chain of events which lead to Matthews being arrested for murdering his second wife.

YUILL, P.B.
English writer

'P.B. Yuill' is the pseudonym of Gordon Williams (born 1939)

 Read on

- *Safely to the Grave* (about the relationship of two boys – one a psychopath – as they grow into adulthood).
- ▷Vera Caspary, *The Man Who Loved His Wife*; ▷Winston Graham, *Marnie*; ▷Ira Levin, *A Kiss Before Dying*.

 Read on

- ▷Dan Kavanagh, *Duffy*; ▷John Milne, *Daddy's Girl*; ▷Dick Francis, *Whip Hand*.

and Terry Venables (born 1943). The Yuill books are stories about James Hazell, a streetwise private eye in the sleazier parts of London. Cockney slang, corkscrew plots, plenty of (often nasty) action, graphically described by cocky, cheery Hazell himself. The series includes *Hazell Plays Solomon*, *Hazell and the Three Card Trick* and *Hazell and the Menacing Jester*.

Gordon Williams' books under his own name include *The Man Who Had Power over Women*, *The Siege of Trencher's Farm/Straw Dogs* and *Walk, Don't Walk*.

MURDERS THEY WROTE –
A GLOSSARY

Caper novel The detailed, minute-by-minute story of how some spectacular crime (usually robbery) is committed. A few caper novels are serious, but most are funny – split-second timing fights human fallibility, and loses.

Golden age The golden ages of detective stories were the 1920s–30s in the USA, and the 1930s–40s in the UK. The golden age of private-eye stories began in the 1940s, and (after a lapse in the 1960s, when spy stories took over) continues today. Thrillers have had two golden ages – the 1940s–50s (adventure thrillers) and the 1960s–80s (spy thrillers, especially East versus West).

Hard-boiled fiction Crime stories where the detective is 'as tough as a 20-minute egg' (to quote ▷Dashiell Hammett's private eye, Sam Spade). The ingredients are clipped language, one-liners, no mushy emotion and plenty of violence. The style peaked in the USA in the 1920s–40s, both in pulp writing and in Hollywood gangster films.In the 1980s and beyond it had a second flowering, especially in the work of ▷Dick Francis and ▷Robert B. Parker.

Locked-room mystery Story in which the crime (usually murder) is committed in circumstances (such as a room locked from the inside) from which the criminal can have had no possible means of escape, and yet is no longer there. To find out who committed the crime, the detective must first work out *how* it was done.

Police procedural Story in which police work is described in careful, minute-by-minute detail. Some police procedurals deal with the investigation of a single crime, but many show the police working on several cases at once.

Private eye Professional sleuth who is not a policeman. So-called because the first US private detective agency, Pinkerton's, had a staring eye as symbol.

Pulp fiction Stories in such magazines as *Black Mask* and *Ellery Queen's Mystery Magazine*, popular in the USA in the 1920s–50s, and cheap novels of the same kind, published as 'paperback originals'. So-called because publishers and authors expected their work to be pulped after use, not kept; they had no designs on lasting fame. Many authors specialized in writing for the pulps, and others (for example ▷Chandler and ▷Hammett) used them as a training ground.

Quest thriller A story in which the hero(es) go on a quest, seeking lost truth, a missing person, or some valuable object, and are beset by crooks, rivals and unexpected developments at every stage.

WHO'S WHO

The first name belongs to the fictional hero, the second name to his or her creator.

Character	Creator
Albany	GODEY
Alleyn	MARSH
Appleby	INNES
Archer	MACDONALD, R.
Argand	RATHBONE
Aubrey	THOMAS, C.
Audley	PRICE
Battle	CHRISTIE
Beck	SJÖWALL and WAHLÖÖ
Beresford	CHRISTIE
Binton	BARTH
Blair	ANDERSON
Blaise	O'DONNELL
Bonaparte	UPFIELD
Bond	FLEMING, GARDNER J.
Bradley	MITCHELL
Bradshaw	DOBYNS
Brandstetter	HANSEN
Brown, Father	CHESTERTON
Brown, Jane and Dagobert	AMES
Brunt	HILTON, J.B.
Burnivel	CANDY
Cadfael	PETERS, ELLIS
Callaghan	CHEYNEY
Campion	ALLINGHAM
Carella	McBAIN
Carrados	BRAMAH

WHO'S WHO

Castang	FREELING
Caution	CHEYNEY
Chambrun	PENTECOST
Charles, Nick and Nora	HAMMETT
Chee	HILLERMAN
Cockrill	BRAND
Coffin	BUTLER
Coffin Ed Johnson	HIMES
Colby	DODGE
Continental Op	HAMMETT
Cooperman	ENGEL
Courtney	SMITH, W.
Crane	LATIMER
Cribb	LOVESEY
Crow	LEWIS
Cuff	COLLINS, W.
Dalgleish	JAMES
Dalziel	HILL
Daniels	BUTLER
Dee, Judge	VAN GULIK
Delaware	KELLERMAN
Deventer	ANDERSON
Dortmunder & Co	WESTLAKE
Dougal	TAYLOR
Duffy	KAVANAGH
Duluth	QUENTIN
Dupin	POE; HARRISON
87th Precinct	McBAIN
Emerson	PETERS, ELIZABETH
Epton	UNDERWOOD
Erridge	STEIN
Fansler Crossan	
Falkenstein	SHANNON
Fell	CARR
Fellows	WAUGH
Felse	PETERS, ELLIS
Fen	CRISPIN
Fletcher	MCDONALD, G.
Flynn	MCDONALD, G.
Fortune	COLLINS, M.
French	CROFTS
Gethryn	MACDONALD, P.
Ghote	KEATING

Gibson	STONE
Gideon	MARRIC
Gordon	EBERSOHN
Grant, Celia	SHERWOOD
Grant, Inspector	TEY
Grant, Patrick	YORKE
Gravedigger Jones	HIMES
Gray	JAMES
Guernaccia	NABB
Hammer	SPILLANE
Hannasyde	HEYER
Hannay	BUCHAN
Harding	HEYER
Hazell	YUILL
Hazelrigg	GILBERT
Helm	HAMILTON
Hemingway	HEYER
Hemlock	TREVANIAN
Holmes	DOYLE
Honeybath	INNES
Hope	McBAIN
Hoyland	MANN
Jenner	MILNE
Johnson	DUNNETT
Kearney	GORES
Kelling	MacLEOD
Kenworthy	HILTON, J.B.
Kramer	McCLURE
Landon	LEWIS
Leaphorn	HILLERMAN
Leithen	BUCHAN
LeVine	BERGMAN
Llorca	AMES
Maddox	BLAISDELL (in USA LININGTON)
Maigret	SIMENON
Mallett	HARE
Mann	SPILLANE
Marlowe	CHANDLER; PARKER
Marple	CHRISTIE
Mason	GARDNER
Masuto	CUNNINGHAM

Maxin	LYALL
McCunn	BUCHAN
McGee	MacDONALD, J.D.
Merrivale	DICKSON
Morse	DEXTER
Muffin	FREEMANTLE
Mulligan and Hunt	STEIN
Murdock	COXE
Noon	AVALLONE
Nur Arslan Bey	RATHBONE
Oakes	GARDNER, J.
O'Breen	BOUCHER
Otani	MELVILLE
Palmer	DEIGHTON
Paris	BRETT
Partanna	CONDON
Peabody	PETERS, ELIZABETH
Peters	KAMINSKY
Pettigrew	HARE
Pibble	DICKINSON
Pink	MOFFAT
Pitt	CUSSLER
Poirot	CHRISTIE
Pollifax	GILMAN
Potter	MALING
Povin	TRENHAILE
Purbright	WATSON
Pym, Inspector	BURLEY
Quantrill	RADLEY
Queen	QUEEN
Quill	BRAHMS and SIMON
Quiller	HALL
Quist	PENTECOST
Reeder	WALLACE
Renko	CRUZ SMITH
Rhodenbarr	BLOCK
Ripley	HIGHSMITH
Russell	HAGGARD
Safford	LATHEN
Saint, The	CHARTERIS

Salter	WRIGHT
Samson, A.	LEWIN
Samson, B.	DEIGHTON
Sargeant	BOX
Schmidt	BAGBY
Scobie	CLEARY
Sessions	WAUGH
Shaft	TIDYMAN
Shandy	MacLEOD
Shard	McCUTCHAN
Shaw	McCUTCHAN
Sheringham	BERKELEY
Shore	FRASER
Small, Rabbi	KEMELMAN
Smiley	LE CARRÉ
Spade	HAMMETT
Spenser	PARKER
Stoner	VALIN
Strangeways	BLAKE, N.
Styles	PHILIPS
Temple	DURBRIDGE
Thatcher	LATHEN
Tibbett	MOYES
Tibbs	BALL
Tobin	COE
Torry	GARDNER J.
Trant	PATRICK
Trent	BENTLEY, E.C.
Ursula, Sister	BOUCHER
Vance	VAN DINE
Van Der Valk	FREELING
Varallo	EGAN
Walker	ESTLEMAN
Ward	LEWIS
Warshawski	PARETSKY
West	CREASEY
Westlake	STAGGE
Wexford	RENDELL
Whitney	DODGE
Willing	McCLOY
Wimsey	SAYERS
Wine	SIMON

WHO'S WHO

Wolfe	STOUT; GOLDSBOROUGH
Wycliffe	BURLEY
Zondi	McCLURE

Index

Athenian Widow, The 72
Atlantic Fury 36, 82
Attending Physician, The 91
Audemars, Pierre 58
Authorized Murder 30
Autumn Tiger 90, 115
Avallone, Michael 5–6, 23, 31, 140, 146
Avenge the Belgrano 7, 61, 90, 133
Avenue of the Dead, The 5
Ax 77, 80
Axwater 18

Babe with the Twistable Arm, The 140
Babson, Marian 1, 11, 24, 47, 52, 55, 72
Babylon South 27
Babysitter, The 27
Bagby, George 115, 140
Bagley, Desmond 7, 82, 85, 97, 115, 138, 146
Bahama Crisis 82
Bailey, H.C. 152, 154
Bait, The 116
Baldwin, James 77
Balkan Assignment, The 124
Ballard, J.G. 54
Ballinger, Bill S. 138
Ball, John 7, 56
Bandit Doctor, The 147
Bandits 93
Banking on Death 90
Bank Shot 10, 157
Banks, Oliver 5, 83
Barboza Credentials, The 43, 97
Bardin, John Franklin 110
Barnard, Robert 8, 64, 72, 96, 113, 137, 155
Barnes, Julian 87
Barnes, Linda 52, 55
Barnett, James 110, 136, 155
Baron and the Beggar, The 32
Baron and the Chinese Puzzle, The 40
Baron Goes A-Buying, The 45
Barrett, G.J. 31
Barth, Richard 20, 115
Base Case 129
Bastard, The 64, 86, 154
Bat Out of Hell 44
Bawden, Nina 81, 144
Baxt, George 29
Bear's Tears, The 28, 145
Beast in View 110
Beast Must Die, The 10
Beauty and the Beast 80
Beauty Sleep 119

Because of the Cats 58
Beckoning Lady, The 2, 8, 104
Bedelia 21, 110
Beeding, Francis 137
Beersheba Triangle 64
Before the Fact 81
Behn, Noel 37
Belladonna 96
Bellairs, George 16
Bellary Bay 157
Bell, Josephine 120
Belshazzar Affair, The 47
Benson, Ben 123
Benson Murder Case, The 46, 132, 152
Bentley, E(dmund) C(lerihew) 8–9, 46, 132, 152
Bentley, Nicolas 100
Benton, Kenneth 47
Bergman, Andrew 9, 12, 69, 86, 125
Berkeley, Anthony 8, 9, 81, 100
Berlin Game 92, 124, 133
Berlin Memorandum, The 38, 149
Bertie and the Seven Bodies 78, 96
Bertie and the Tin Man 96
Best Families, The 40
Beware of the Trains 33
Beware the Curves 60
Beyond Hope 52
Beyond This Point Are Monsters 110
Biafra Story, The 57
Big Caper, The 17
Big Foot 95
Bigger They Come, The 60
Big Gold Dream, The 77
Big Kiss-off of 1944, The 9, 69, 125
Big Knockover, The 70
Big Man 79
Big Midget Murders, The 13
Big Money 10
Big Shot 123
Big Sleep, The 21, 22
Billion Dollar Killing, The 50, 53, 103
Billion Dollar Sure Thing, The 50, 53, 103
Bimbos of the Death Sun 30
Bingham, John 110, 137
Binyon, T.J. 65
Birthday Deathday 120
Bishop Murder Case, The 9, 152
Bishop's Crime, The 152
Bismarck Herrings 111
Bitter Medicine 50, 88, 118
Black, Gavin 150

INDEX

INDEX

INDEX

INDEX